From High Heels to High Hills

From High Heels to High Hills

One woman walking the Lake District – in her own style

Tanya Oliver

First published in Great Britain in 2012 by Step Beach Press, Brighton

Copyright © Tanya Oliver

The right of Tanya Oliver to be identified as the author of the work has been asserted by her in accordance with the Copyright, Designs and Patents Act 1988.

A CIP catalogue record for this title is available from the British Library.

ISBN 978 1 908779 02 1

Typeset in Turners Hill, UK by Christine Gardner
Cover design by Christine Gardner
Photographs by Tanya Oliver

Edited by Jo Hathaway

Printed in Europe. Manufactured and managed by Jellyfish Solutions

Step Beach Press, 28 Osborne Villas, Hove, East Sussex BN3 2RE

www.stepbeachpress.co.uk

Note: This book reflects the author's personal experiences and recommendations about fell walking. It is, of course, entirely the individual's responsibility to prepare fully for fell-walking.

To Peter G –
for helping me have the strength to
believe and the courage to go for it!

Contents

Acknowledgements

There are so many people I would like to thank even if they do not know they have helped me. I am sure I will miss some people out but please know that I am very grateful for all the input, support and inspiration I have received.

First my family – Paul, who has battled his way up mountains in sun, wind, mist and snow all because I have a dream, and my mum and dad for introducing me to the Lakes and for all the lifts they gave me.

My friends, particularly Christy Holden for the Dune shoes, and Chloe Greene, Peter Gilroy and Jane Kendal for their unswerving support. All my friends have been supportive of my blog and change of career, however, and for that I thank you all.

The Online Fell Walking Club (OFC) founded in 2001 by Peter Burgess. It has been great reading and being inspired by your walking stories and thank you for all the tips on some of the things I did not know about the Lakes and for your support on the blog and book.

Some of my Twitter followers have been superb both in the things they have said and the information and insights they have given me. Thank you to all those who have supported my blog, retweeted my tweets and engaged in interesting conversations. If you could support the book too that would be great!

My editor at Step Beach, Jo Hathaway for her brilliant suggestions and comments (and being gentle in the process!).

Ray Greenhow for his support and insights to the Lake District.

Alfred Wainwright (1907–1991) for giving the world a wonderful set of 'Pictorial Guides of Lakeland'.

All the wonderful pubs, restaurants and cafés I have had the pleasure to visit and hotels and self-catering properties I have stayed in.

Introduction

'The things that make me different are the things that make me, "me".
                                     Winnie-the-Pooh (A. A. Milne, 1928)

I looked up at the ascent of Jack's Rake again with my bruised arms and knees already feeling sore. If I am honest, I was actually very scared. What on earth was I doing here? And why on my own? What was I thinking? I am not a rock-climber and have never wanted to be one. This danger was entirely self-inflicted. At that moment I would have gladly traded my walking boots for heels and a glass of champagne somewhere. Going back down was not an option so I had to keep going. Again I took some deep breaths to steady my nerves and looked up at the rocks in front of me. (See Chapter Seven: My Favourite Fells (Part II) to see how this turns out…)

I must be the only person who, when packing for a hiking trip to the Lake District, packs three pairs of high heels 'just in case'. Well honestly, you just never know! Tucked right alongside the heels though are a pair of sturdy and robust hiking boots.

I am Kentish born and bred and now live in Sussex, so I am truly southern. However, for many holidays when I was growing up we headed north to the Lake District and I loved it. My great grandmother on my mum's side used to travel to the Lake District to paint, so my family has a long association with the area. I will confess that between the ages of 7 and 14, climbing mountains was hardly my first choice of activity. My mum and dad must have been saints listening to the constant tirade of 'Are we nearly there yet?' and 'This is sooooo steep!' But I always got to the top and when up there, forgot how hateful the climb was and loved being on top of the world. I must have got the bug somehow, despite my protestations, as now I am an adult, climbing mountains is my addiction.

So why do I do it? Climbing mountains is hard work and even though I am quite fit, sometimes, on the way up, I will admit to feeling that it is a real strain and effort to get to the next milestone. At these moments, I have what I call 'view stops'. Even without needing a break though, one of the main points of climbing mountains for me is the views. The Lake District is beautiful and looks stunning at any level – from your car, the tops of buses or on low-level walks. But when up in the mountains, the views are, quite simply, spectacular – even on a wet or misty day there is something eerie and mystical about them. Wordsworth and Coleridge captured some of the magic and romance of the Lakes in their poems, and I can see how they fell in love with them.

Mystical Wastwater.

I read a book recently by Alastair Lee called 'Lake District Mountain Landscape' (2010) and something he said rang true for me:

'Much of the fells' subtle beauty derives from their soft, more intimate human scale, compared to higher mountains.'

Whilst I can admire the scale of the Himalayas and other major mountain ranges, I have no desire to climb them (although I always find it interesting to read about others that have). The mountains in the Lake District are older than the ranges in Europe,

America and Asia, which I had not realised. Apparently they used to be in league with the Himalayas (about half a billion years ago!) but have worn down over time. How amazing is that?

The views around Wastwater are probably my favourite overall. They bring back memories of happy childhood days sitting in the river that feeds the lake, and of going out onto the little island with a picnic. I have always found the screes at Wastwater awe-inspiring and a little scary (in a good way). Combined with Great Gable, Yewbarrow and the Scafells, I believe the area is one of nature's most magical.

Wastwater screes.

I climbed Yewbarrow from Overbeck Bridge in January 2011. This is one of my all time favourite climbs for many reasons, including the rugged terrain and the fact you gain height quickly, which I prefer. It was a beautiful sunny winter's day with some snow on the surrounding higher peaks but not on Yewbarrow itself. The snow looked like a glossy meringue. I had been climbing for about an hour and the views looking back were of ever-increasing beauty. Then, as I emerged onto the ridge, the view simply took my breath away. Wastwater was glistening below in the sunshine and was as still as ice, with the dark, eerie screes rising behind with an almost menacing magic. The screes reflected in the still water as though you could almost see them reach the bottom of the lake. To the left, the Scafells towered over all neighbouring heights with a natural dominance and Great Gable stood proudly at the head of the valley with a majesty all of its own. There was not a cloud in the sky. This then, was heaven. As I stood and looked in wonder, I felt an emotion rise within me that almost brought me to tears. You cannot imagine it unless you have seen it. Here, on this fell, without a soul around I felt I could look at that view forever and that there was nothing in the world that could take this feeling away. Everything felt just right. It was simply magic. Except it was all real.

Whilst this book is light-hearted, I am a serious fell walker. I have been walking in the Lakes for years. The most popular and famous guides are those written more than 60 years ago by Alfred Wainwright. He compiled a series of 'Pictorial Guides to the Lakeland Fells' between 1954 and 1965, which were revised recently by Chris Jesty (2005–2009). In these guides, Wainwright wrote about 214 fells, which are now commonly referred to as 'the Wainwright's'. I have completed all the Wainwright's and intend to do many of them time and time again. I have climbed many non-Wainwright fells as well. Over half the mountains I have climbed I have climbed alone, others with my husband, Paul, my mum and dad, and friends. But I have a truly independent streak. I have climbed in fair weather and foul, baking sun and freezing ice. I have skipped across grassy plains and dragged myself out of muddy bogs. (Here, I admit a failing that I sometimes get so caught up in the views that I forget the cardinal rule to watch where I am putting my feet!) When I climbed Seat Sandal in December 2010, not only did my water freeze in the bottles but my hair was crunchy with ice by the time I got to the top. It was one of my favourite climbs though.

As I say, I am addicted to climbing mountains – climbing mountains... and high-heeled shoes. The girly side of me is strong. My friends find it hard to imagine me going from smart outfits and posh heels to waterproofs and walking boots. However, when I show them pictures they do admit I do it in style in a combination of colours but with a major focus on pink. You can climb mountains in style and have all the practical and weather-proof equipment you need. My style slips a little when I trip or stumble, when it is hot and my cheeks are rosy, or windy and my hair is caught in my lip balm. Fortunately, I get to choose the photos I include in the book! I am not All Walker. I am not a fitness fanatic, I find it hard to drag myself to the gym when I am at home (and consequently do not go as often as I should), and I am not a hardened rock climber using grappling irons (I could not fit them in my rucksack with all the clothes

My boots and heels.

Dressed for a walk in Sussex.

and lipstick anyway). I am an ordinary walker and have no wish to be anything else. I simply love climbing mountains and I want to encourage others to do the same – it is great fun and great exercise. It is not all about mountains though, there is much more to the Lake District that I will also touch on (and there is nothing like a nice spa day after climbing a few fells).

Chapter One: What the Guide Books Do Not Tell You

This is not a guide book. Not by any stretch of the imagination. But I want to start with what the proper guide books *don't* tell you about climbing mountains. I love reading guide books but they always make it sound straightforward and you run the risk of thinking you are the only one that actually (in truth) gets out of breath on the way up. Well, let me assure you that you are not! To me, being *able* to climb a mountain is one thing – the guide books tell you where to start and finish, the route in between and what to expect about the terrain and what you're looking at while you're doing it. I want to talk about how it actually *feels* to climb a mountain. I have taken years to gather first-hand knowledge and I feel I can speak with confidence. By passing on these insights, I hope to add context to the technicalities of maps and guide books that I love.

Striking a pose on the "lion" of Helm Crag.

Brace yourself...

1. The point of the mountain you are looking at that you *think* is the top *never* is. There are always one, two or three more 'tops' to climb before you get to the true summit. In other words it is always further than you think. As Wainwright said, fell-walking and wishful thinking have nothing in common!

2. The shortcut is rarely quicker as it usually turns out to be much steeper (although the longer route always seems very steep anyway so you can't win!) Despite knowing this, I continue time after time to take the 'shortcut'.

3. If there are two paths to choose from, invariably, the path you need is the steep and uninviting one, not the gentle sloping one.

4. The wind is *always* against you. No matter how many times you change direction. This is, of course, unless (for girls and guys with long hair) you decide to put your hair up. At this moment the wind becomes a whirlwind from all directions so there are always strands or chunks that escape and flap around your eyes or get stuck in your lip balm.

5. However steep you think a particular climb is going to be it always feels steeper than you think (whatever the map contours say), or, if you have done it before, steeper than you remember.

6. Just when you think you cannot possibly go any further, that whoever thought of climbing mountains must be seriously deluded and you are staggering to your 15th view stop, someone around the age of 80 will stroll pass you, making it look like a doddle.

But it is worth it because...

1. No matter how good the views are, there are nearly always better ones further on.

2. You will get to the top – it is possible, however hard you are breathing and how much your legs hurt on the way up and however much you feel like giving up! If they're honest, *everyone* feels like that at some point.

3. Whatever the pain of ascent, you will forget it the moment you reach the top and marvel at the wonder of being on top of the world (I gather they say this about child birth but I am not in a position to comment).

4. When you get back down, there is nothing in the world as good as a shandy, glass of wine or hot chocolate (whatever your tipple of choice) as you contemplate what you have achieved.

5. Unless you break a limb on the way up or down, mountain climbing is seriously good for you and will get the endorphins going. Even more than chocolate!

As I said, you will not get these tips in your standard guide book so use this as an addendum to your map or book of choice and rest assured that you are not alone if these things happen to you.

A few basics: what you always wanted to know about physical geography and were afraid to ask!

One of the things that can be a bit bewildering as you start out on the Whole Walking Business is getting to grips with the terminology and the terrain. An Ordnance Survey map (or equivalent) is pretty much essential and with a bit of guidance and practice, you'll soon learn to follow them. However, to get you started, I've given a few basic definitions in the table opposite.

Some advice on what to take while climbing

At this point I should say that my high heels do not make it into my rucksack (although there was a question mark over this when I climbed the Fairfield Horseshoe). They have not done so yet anyway, but I continue to search for the opportunity to combine heels and hills more effectively.

I have been climbing for most of my life so can speak from experience (although I miss the days when I was little and my dad used to carry the rucksack); the most seasoned walker can be caught unawares by the change in weather, dangerous crags or slippery rocks so it is essential to take care. I am fortunate that I have never had to call on the services of the Mountain Rescue teams and it is beholden on us all to be careful so we do not have to. They do an outstanding job, all on a voluntary basis, but are woefully under-resourced so do not take them for granted. It is important to treat mountains with respect.

My tips for safe climbing

1. As Wainwright said: **Watch where you are putting your feet**. It is easy to get subsumed by the views but do not get carried away.

2. If you possibly can, take a **GPS (Global Positioning System)**. I started using one in December 2010 and have never looked back. In mist, they are invaluable. Some walkers think it is heresy to have a GPS – I disagree completely (see Chapter Eight: Getting Lost! to find out why).

3. Yes I am an advocate of GPS but I always have an **Ordnance Survey map and a compass** with me and usually a Wainwright guide as well. If you do take the trouble to take an OS map and compass, make sure you know how to use them, particularly if your GCSE or O-Level geography days were a long time ago!

4. **Tell someone where you are going**. I usually do self-catering so there is no one locally I can tell. So I have a system with my dad, even though he is in Kent – I text him to tell him where I am going and what time I am going to start, and at various points where I have signal on the route. Then when I get back (as soon as I have reception) I text him to say I am safely down. If he had not heard from me by the time it starts to get dark, he would raise the alert and know approximately where I was.

Term	Definition	What it means for you!
Fell	A barren or stony hill	Mountain – takes a lot of effort to get to the top but worth it when you do!
Ridge	The long narrow top of a mountain or group of mountains	A triumph and some good views (the latter being weather dependent!)
Ghyll/gill	A rocky stream or river on a mountain	Admire and take photos but avoid falling in (like I did once) unless you wish to try 'gill scrambling', the very purpose of which is to climb/jump/scramble down gills!
Bog	An area of ground that is always wet and soft	Potential trouble! This is when you get to test your footwear and your waterproofs. Undignified if you fall in (see Chapter Four: Bogs and Screes)
Crag	Rocky outcrops on mountains (sometimes included in the name of mountains ie. Eagle Crag)	Admire and avoid unless you are a rock climber!
Scree	A slope covered with small pieces of rock; small loose pieces of broken rock at the bottom of a cliff or along the slopes of a mountain	Much energy will be exerted in the two steps forward, one step back approach unless you have good grip!
Tarn	A mountain lake or pool	A joy to look at – pretty and a good lunch spot or place to paddle (you can even swim in some)
Gully	A small or large ravine, often caused by water but sometimes by footpath erosion	Avoid unless it forms part of an official route
Cairn	A pile of stones that marks the top of the mountain (and sometimes the route up or down)	Either: You've made it! Or: Good news – you are actually on a path of some description!
Col	The low point between mountains or ridges	The dip in between mountains (chance to get your breath back!)
Packhorse bridge	Stone bridge with low arches originally constructed for the use of pack horses carrying loads	Quaint little bridges over pretty streams – photo opportunity!
Force (as in Stockghyll Force)	Waterfall	Lovely part of a mountain walk if you are lucky enough to pass one

(Definitions of 'fell', 'ridge', 'scree', 'bog', 'cairn', and 'ghyll' taken from www.macmillandictionary.com; definition of 'tarn', 'crag', 'force', 'packhorse bridge', 'col' and 'gully' are author's own.)

5. **Do not take unnecessary risks**. You will see from my stories that I have climbed in all sorts of weather. I do that as I am confident in my GPS and in my sensible approach and I have lots of experience. I am never complacent, however, and there have been times when I have decided it is too late, too misty or just too risky to continue and have turned around or taken an exit-route. It can be soul-destroying when you have come so far but better that than broken limbs or worse.

6. **Take waterproofs** – even when it is sunny when you start. Good quality ones that are genuinely waterproof and not 'water-resistant' or 'shower-proof'. Trust me, there is a difference! Even if it does not rain on the journey, they are another useful tool against the wind and cold as the temperatures can surprise you at the top. I have not yet found a glamorous alternative to waterproof over-trousers sadly but I remain optimistic.

7. **Take a First Aid kit** – I include plasters, blister plasters (which are absolutely amazing), one of the antibacterial hand gels, bandages, mini scissors, bite cream, hayfever tablets, ibuprofen and moisturiser. That is just me though – there may be other things you need.

8. This one may sound excessive and I have never used it but always take it with me – a **hypothermia bag** (which looks like a large foil bag that you get into to keep warm). You just never know and if you injure yourself and you cannot communicate with anyone, you do not know how long you will be out there for.

9. **Make sure you have suncream and a hat** in the summer as, if you are lucky and it is sunny, there is often little shade (NB please do try and avoid unsightly sock marks from suntan/burn).

10. **Remember to take a torch** – even if you plan to be back down well before darkness falls; if you have an accident or get lost, you may be out there longer than you thought. I have a head torch so I can keep my hands free.

11. It's worth having some **spare bootlaces** (also useful if you forget 12, below).

12. One for the girls or guys with long hair – **hair bands!** Whilst the cold can surprise you, so too can how hot it gets, even on a cold day when walking. It can also be a safety device – to keep your hair out of your eyes in the wind!

13. Take **water** – lots of it, again, even when it is cold. I personally do not like replenishing my water supply from streams on the way so I take more than enough, but I have seen plenty of people do that!

14. **Think about food** – you will need enough not just for lunch, but also to snack on the way – when your legs start to feel tired, it is amazing what a boost an apple or banana can give; also, try some of the high energy options like Kendal Mint Cake.

15. If it is winter, I always have a **snood, warm hat and thick gloves**. I actually take the hat and gloves with me in the summer as well and have used them on occasion when it has been chilly on the top. I also take thin gloves with me in the summer

because they are useful for moments when you have to scramble – I may love fell-walking but I also like having nice fingernails! They were invaluable when I made my way down the Dore-Head scree (missing the nice green path next to it!)

16. In winter, wear **thermals** – no, they are not glamorous and definitely avoid being seen in them early on in a relationship, but they are essential when walking.

17. Make sure you have a **fully charged mobile phone**.

18. Take **spare batteries** for your torch, GPS and any other gadget you may be using.

19. Finally, you will need a reliable **Sherpa** to carry it all for you! Or failing that, a good quality **waterproof rucksack** (with the waterproof lining that goes over it when it is really tipping it down).

My trusty rucksack.

With all that you will not go far wrong!

Planning your route

My last piece of proper advice is about planning your route and the time it takes to complete it. (If you are a seasoned fell walker then skip to Chapter Two at this point.)

Climbing fells is not the same as walking in flat areas or low hills. It takes longer and is more strenuous to climb, owing to the gradients, terrain and weather (which change all the time). One of the most common formulas for calculating how long a walk will take is **Naismith's Rule**, which was devised by a Scottish mountaineer called W.W. Naismith in 1892. This formula states:

'A fit person will travel an average of five kilometres per hour and will take an extra 30 minutes for every 300 metres of ascent.'

('A Wainwright: A Walker's Notebook', 2007)

This, however, is not an exact science and you will only start to become more accurate by trial and error and understanding your own fitness level.

When planning the route, do pay attention to contours on the map and check whether they are inclines or declines. It sounds obvious but I doubt I am the only one who has got it wrong. I learned the lesson quickly though! The most critical point is that if you have not climbed mountains before, be realistic about what you can achieve – you will not become a fell-runner or SAS navigator overnight. I went ice-skating in New York once with someone who had never been ice-skating before. He thought he could rival Torvill and Dean the moment he stepped on the ice, however, and would master spins and twists in minutes simply because he used to roller skate a lot when younger. He spent most of his time sprawled out flat on the ice though (I spent most of the time chuckling at the edge as it was hilarious to watch!). This shows what misplaced confidence can do! Be sensible and know your limits.

I do not apply the same rule to high heels. With those, limits are there to be tested!

What to wear – combining fells with clothes, shopping and make-up

I know what you're thinking – sensible and stylish cannot, surely, co-exist in the same kagool?! But oh yes, it can be done! I have a whole wardrobe of clothes for climbing in the Lake District – the overriding colour that features is pink because, to quote Reese Witherspoon's character in the film Legally Blonde, pink 'is not just a colour. It is a state of mind'. It is true in my view. Pink is a cheerful colour but it also holds a practical purpose whether you are climbing or walking in summer or winter as if you fall or get lost or have an accident of some sort, it is a good colour to stand out against snow, rocks, grass or any other terrain you may find yourself on (assuming you avoid Flamingo parks).

Serious fell-walkers may find all this a bit girly, but I make no apology for that – I am what I am! I have a pink raincoat for the summer and a pink ski jacket for the winter, along with a white ski jacket with pink detail (I have only ever been skiing once and was more a fan of the après-ski than the *act*ual-ski but the skiing sections of outdoor clothes shops are useful for winter fell-walking too). For those times of fabulous sunshine I also have a pink sun hat and a pink winter hat. My trousers are green khaki-type trousers with lots of pockets for lip balm, hair bands, mobile phone etc.

I love shopping for outdoor clothes almost as much as heels and I see no reason at all why you cannot climb in style. I have not climbed a mountain in heels yet (although I saw a pair of Stilletto Hiking Boots in Harvey Nichols that could have worked a treat!). However, I have managed to combine shopping with climbing on Fleetwith Pike: if you park in the Honister Slate Mine carpark it is £5 for all day but you get that back if you spend £10 in the shop. What is a girl to do? Clearly, the moment I got back down I headed to the shop and purchased some slate gifts (coasters and key rings) and some quirky jewellery – a pretty pink necklace of polished stones and matching bracelet. So shopping and fells can be combined and I aim to find further ways of doing this. If someone could open up a shop that sells heels and outdoor clothing that would be great.

High heels: an extreme sport?

Anyone for skiing?   *Lipstick and mascara – essential walking gear.*

A mountain climber? Really?

Make-up can also be combined with walking. I do not wear a lot of make-up but I cannot go anywhere without mascara. One of my closest friends once told me my eyes were one of my best features so for many years I have worn mascara, particularly since I began wearing contact lenses rather than glasses (which then opened a whole new world of shopping involving sunglasses!). I digress.

I also use waterproof mascara even though it is more difficult to take off in the evenings (or usually in the mornings for me as I can rarely be bothered before I go to bed) as you never know when you are going to get caught in a rain shower or when a scene from a film (or even an episode of Masterchef) will catch you unawares.... I confess I can be a little emotional. When I climb mountains, therefore, I wear mascara. I usually add lipstick as well (although on a sunny day it does tend to melt in the rucksack!). To some it may sound strange to put make-up on to climb a mountain, but why not? When I get back down to the car, before I go into any pub, café or bar I top-up the lipstick and add face powder (no blusher required owing to either heat, cold or a wind-burnt complexion!).

I also change my clothes. You may think I have lost the plot but unless I am absolutely exhausted and do not have the energy to undo a boot lace I change from my walking clothes to something more refined (this could be anything from summer skirts to jeans) combined with either flip-flops or heels or sometimes trainers. There are only a handful of occasions where I have not done this, the most recent being having completed the Wainwright's and not getting to the pub at Wasdale Head until nearly 7pm. Other than these occasions, if you saw me in a pub or café after a walk, you would imagine I was someone who visited the Lakes to sip champagne and stroll in flip-flops between shops or around tarns and had never been up a mountain in my life – there is nothing wrong at all with people who come to the Lakes to do just that, but appearances can be deceptive.

I try and keep my fingernails intact and sometimes wear gloves at rocky points for this reason, plus I wear nail polish on my toes. I discovered a marvellous polish on a spa day in Kent with a friend last year that is a vibrant pink (of course). I wore it climbing my final five Wainwright's and it did not chip. A miracle polish and I wore flip flops for the rest of the week without having to redo my toes. Excellent.

My point really is that you do not have to be a naturally 'outdoorsy' type to climb a mountain in the Lake District. I like my creature comforts and you will not catch me camping until they invent an en-suite and mini bar (not forgetting central heating). You may surprise yourself how much you enjoy being out and about anyway.

Now, we are ready to walk.

Chapter Two: Divided by a Common Language

As you know by now, I am Kentish born and bred and now live in Sussex. I love those two counties but it makes me very southern (for me 'The North' starts somewhere above the M4) and I sound very southern. This is very apparent in the Lake District where pronunciations are a constant source of surprise to me and I, with my attempts at mastering a more northern dialect, am a constant source of entertainment for locals.

An example is the hamlet of Watendlath, near Keswick. Now, all my life I have pronounced this in true southern-style as 'what-end-*larth*', with the emphasis on 'larth' and yes inserting the letter 'r'. My friend Malcolm, who was born and bred in the Lakes and actually grew up near Watendlath, fell about laughing when I said it. After he recovered (about 10 minutes later) he told me how it is actually pronounced – 'wat-*end*-l'th' with the emphasis on 'end' and with a few letters missing. How is someone as southern as me supposed to get that? It is like 'Threshwaite' being pronounced 'Thresh'et'. You are supposed to know things like this in order to avoid sounding daft (a trap I have not avoided – far from it!) One of my Christmas presents was a mini book entitled 'Cumbrian English' – I have perused this at length and am ever hopeful that I will one day get it right!

There are also complications with places being called the same names. There are two villages called Troutbeck very near each other, several Sour Milk Gills and Mosedales, two Red Pikes, two Harter Fells and many Eagle Crags, as well as at least two Red Tarns. It is a minefield of complications that newcomers are bound to fall foul of from time to time. Rest assured, however, this is perfectly normal and there is usually a friendly soul to help you out!

This brings me to the names of mountains. They are just fantastic! Some, like the Buttermere Red Pike and Stone Arthur look like they sound. Other names are very poetic and descriptive, such as Catbells and Haystacks. There are also those that take their names from the surrounding rivers or valleys, like Illgill Head. And then there are those mountains that seem to be named totally randomly but are just wonderful names. I have looked into the meanings of some place names using online search engines and a book by David Watson (2009) called '*Making sense of the place names of the Lake District*'. My favourites are:

Hartsop 'Hart' in Cumbria translates as 'deer' and the word 'sop' means valley, therefore the small hamlet of Hartsop means the 'valley of the deer'.

Yewbarrow I never saw a Yew tree on the way up it! It is conceivable that the top looks like an upturned wheelbarrow (albeit a rather bumpy, well-used one) but that is probably not

The Skiddaw Range – definite mountains.

The Froswick Range – definite mountains.

If it looks like a mountain, it is a mountain. Or is it?

the first description that would spring to mind. If you look at Old English, Yew probably means 'sheep' and barrow 'hill' so that effectively means it is the 'hill where sheep graze' – that and the other 213 fells as I do not think I have been on a fell where there are not sheep grazing somewhere! One of the most striking parts of Yewbarrow is a crag called 'Bell Rib' – this translates from the French word 'Bell' meaning beautiful and the Old English word 'Rib', which refers to the shape. So 'beautiful rib' – not something anyone has ever said to me!

Great Cock-Up Well, I mean, who could resist putting that on the list? What is that name about? Did nature make a mistake when this mountain was created? In my view it is the most amusing mountain name in the Lake District if perhaps not the prettiest! There is no definitive answer about where the fell name comes from but some sources suggest it stems from the Old English words 'cocc' (woodcock) and 'hop' (secluded

valley), therefore 'valley of the woodcock' and the word Great being included to denote it is higher than its neighbouring fell Little Cock-Up (I promise I am not making this up!). Secluded valley is certainly apt as it is the northern fells and you can walk there for hours without meeting another soul.

Catbells One of the most popular mountains for climbers of all ages and an iconic part of the Keswick and Derwent Water scenery. It literally translates as 'the bell-shaped hill where wild cats are found'. I have seen no evidence of wild cats there mind you, which is rather a relief!

Haystacks I need look for no reference for this mountain. When you look at Haystacks, it quite clearly resembles old-fashioned stacks of hay before hay was packed into neat rectangular or circular bales. A perfect name for an attractive fell.

Bannerdale Crags I do not think the word 'Bannerdale' is particularly attractive but I think its meaning is. The word 'banner' means 'holly' and 'dale' is 'valley' therefore Bannerdale is the 'valley of holly' and Bannerdale Crags would be 'the crags in the valley of holly'. I think a valley of holly sounds simply lovely! That said, I have climbed Bannerdale Crags from Bannerdale and I did not see any holly so that is rather disappointing! Just like I have never seen deer in the 'Valley of the Deer' (but I know they are there and will continue to look!)

Mellbreak I had to include this as one of my favourite mountains but the meaning is not entirely clear. The best guess is that it is a Gaelic word that possibly means 'dappled hill'. That seems to fit – the fell is dappled with crags and heather and sections of scree. At various points it is probably dappled with people having view stops too!

Ullscarf I include this mountain name as it refers to 'the pass of wolves'. Wolves used to roam the fells and valleys of the Lake District but have been gone from there for many years and therefore the mountains of the Lake District, unlike many of the mountain areas in the USA for example, are predator-free as far as people are concerned. There are many dangers when walking and climbing but being mauled by a wolf or bear is not one of them I am glad to say!

Loughrigg I will end with this name as it is such a popular sight. It is easily translated with 'lough' meaning 'lake' and 'rig' meaning 'ridge', therefore Loughrigg is 'the ridge by the lake'. Extremely apt I would say!

There are many different interpretations of place and fell names and my research showed there is little agreement on the derivation of some of them. I do not claim that all these are accurate – it is simply a bit of fun!

Then there is the question of how you define a mountain. Now, I have pondered this for some time. When is a mountain not a mountain? Frankly, I have no idea. I am a massive Wainwright fan and extol the virtues of his guide book series to all and sundry. He is part of the reason I love the Lake District. I have climbed not just the 214 Wainwright's but several other mountains as well.

And therein lies my point. How is a mountain defined? When is a mountain not a mountain? It seems quite arbitrary to me in many ways. How can somewhere as flat, with such little resemblance to a mountain and with such few metres of height between it and its neighbour be a mountain, yet something that has many more metres between its neighbour and itself and frankly look more like a mountain should, not be classed as a separate fell? I am thinking first and foremost of Mungrisdale Common near Blencathra (those of you who have been there will understand what I mean), which in my view is flat and dull and indistinguishable from the route to Blencathra. How can this be a separate fell when Stile End between Barrow and Outside, which has clear sides and height from its neighbours and looks like a mountain should (pointy) is not? Another example is that Armboth Fell (second only to Mungrisdale Common in my list of fells to be avoided) is a mountain but the towering, larger, more distinguished Bell Crags, but a stone's throw away, is not? The latest Cicerone guide for this area has Bell Crag as a separate fell so even the experts do not always agree.

Nab Scar seems just a part of Heron Pike to me as part of the Fairfield Horseshoe and Stone Arthur is virtually indistinguishable as part of the route to Blea Rigg (although the rocky top is distinctive from Grasmere). Broad Crag and Ill Crag near Scafell Pike are both over 3,000 feet/914 metres but neither are classed as separate fells. I could go on.

It seems very random to me. I am sure there are technical explanations but I doubt they will convince me so I will maintain the view that it is more arbitrary than anything else. Whilst I will continue to be a huge Wainwright fan, I disagree with some of the judgments in his 214 fells. I will still look upon Mungrisdale Common as a flat marsh that is merely a part of Blencathra, as Armboth Fell as the devil's own work and a part of Bell Crags and Stile End as a cracking little fell in its own right.

Chapter Three: Ridge Walks

One of the wonderful things about walking in the Lake District is that once you have climbed one fell, you can usually walk for miles and miles across the ridges to other fells and see a myriad other views. Even if it is not strictly a ridge, there are several fells you can do without losing or gaining too much height in between. It feels like you are on top of the world and it is just wonderful. On these routes you often find silent pretty tarns, rocky ridges, grassy paths and imposing crags. You can see the sea from some fells and as far as Scotland and the Isle of Man. Or you can be looking towards beautiful blue lakes with striking mountains behind in one direction and rolling grassy hills the other. It can take your breath away. There are many classic examples of this, such as the Hellvelyn Range, Fairfield Horseshoe, Mosedale Horseshoe and the High Street range. Walks like this are exhilarating and even though they can be tiring, they are well worth the effort.

I use a range of guides to plan these routes, as well as Wainwright books and Ordnance Survey maps. Two of my most used resources at the moment are the Fellranger guides by Cicerone and the walking maps by walkingbooks.com. There are plenty of other tools out there as well, including the highly innovative 'Tubular Fells' map by Peter Burgess that uses the distinctive London Underground map to connect the fells.

Here are some of my favourite ridge walks.

The Buttermere Range

This was my first planned ridge walk in the Lake District back in June 2010 as part of climbing the Wainwright's. It was a beautiful day with a clear blue sky and bright sunshine but it was not overly hot – idyllic climbing conditions! To get the best from the walk, the route I planned first took in the shore path of Lake Buttermere through the wood from the National Trust car park near the Fish Hotel and then over High Crag, High Stile and Red Pike. There are two Red Pikes in the Lake District – this one at Buttermere and the other is at Wasdale.

It was a gentle stroll for about two miles and very picturesque. If you are not keen on getting up on the fells there is enough beauty and interest in all the lakes and tarns to satisfy anyone. I was already really enjoying the walk and then, as I emerged from the woods, the path began to strike out inevitably upwards towards the first fell – High Crag. It was steep and rocky in places but nothing difficult and the views opening up across the lake and towards Fleetwith Pike and Haystacks to the left were striking. Haystacks was Wainwright's favourite mountain and it is near Innominate Tarn that his ashes were scattered after his death.

You may remember what I said about the shortcut versus the longer routes. In my experience, the shortcut is rarely quicker, however tempting it looks and my advice is to think carefully before opting for short and steep over longer and less steep. However, as I rarely take my own advice, I decided to opt for the shortcut. The longer route would have taken me up to Scarth Gap but I decided on the shortcut that took the hypotenuse across the diagonal rather than the right angle (…thought I would throw in some GCSE mathematics to show I learned more than geography and history when I was at school and to prove to my children if I ever have any that maths actually is a useful subject to learn as you use it your whole life!). Off I went across a grassy field that frankly did not look like it had a path to me and was seriously steep! I had to stop a lot to rest my legs and the wall at the top did not seem to be getting any closer. I made a mental note to myself not to take the shortcut ever again (which I then promptly spent the next few years ignoring).

Eventually I reached the ridge with tired legs – how on earth was I going to do another two mountains after this one? I must be crazy! People do this for fun? The last 90 metres of ascent was also steep and up a path that wound its way between areas of scree. As I made my way up the path, I looked up and racing towards me down the scree was a fell-runner! Yes – there are people that run up and down fells! This guy was fair tearing down the scree and looked like he could fall and break his leg or his neck at any moment but he got to the foot of the scree without mishap and kept on his way as I looked after him with my mouth gaping open. He was followed over a period of five or six minutes by another 20 or so fell-runners – all of whom looked like they would surely kill themselves but who all made it down successfully. Some people wonder why I climb mountains – they simply do not get it. I, in turn, wonder not just how but why people would want to be running on mountains? Is it not hard enough just walking? I absolutely do not understand it but they have my total respect as their fitness levels and stamina must be immense. Each to their own!

The fell-runners distracted me for a while and before I knew it I had reached the summit of High Crag and was rewarded with glorious views across Buttermere and to the fells behind Robinson and the Dale Head range, to Fleetwith Pike and Haystacks with Great Gable beyond and then towards my next fell – High Stile. One of the most amazing things about the Lake District is how small it actually is, as the crow flies. To drive to Wastwater from Buttermere would take upwards of an hour. However, Great Gable, which looked so close, has its foot in the Wasdale valley. Amazing.

The ridge to High Stile was a joyous skip with very little effort and a chance to just keep soaking up the views and the sunshine. The view to Red Pike from High Stile showed very clearly how Red Pike got its name as it has red soil surrounding the top, which is Syenite and igneous rock red in appearance and is particularly obvious where the mountain has eroded. There was also the first view of Bleaberry Tarn in the hollow below. Red Pike has two 'tops' and from the village of Buttermere, you can only see the lower one, which most people assume is the true top. It is not until you are nearly upon it that you realise it is not and there is a further ascent. From my route however, again, it was just a simple and beautiful ridge walk.

The Buttermere Range reflected in Buttermere.

The summit of Red Pike was crowded as it is one of the more popular fells to climb. As I made my way down the rather treacherous route (well-worn from many a pair of boots before me), I was very conscious that a misplaced foot could see me fall backwards into the red earth – this would not look good on my trousers as I was not sure the red/green combination would be a good one! There was a woman coming up who looked like she had been over a few times and she looked exhausted. She was determined to get to the top though – good on her!

The route down was very tiring as a lot of it was rocky steps and they jarred a lot – it was by far the most unrelenting descent of my walks so far. The walk past Bleaberry Tarn was utterly beautiful though and made me forget even how tired my limbs were. The path soon entered the woods by the lake and rejoined the path I had begun that morning. I can honestly say this is one of the best ridge walks I have ever done and I would recommend it for those just starting out on serious fell-walking.

The Langdale Pikes Saga – If at first you don't succeed...

Climbing the Langdale Pikes in the Lake District is something probably thousands of people do every year. I had thought this would be one of the most straightforward as they are close together and, compared to some of the southern fells, are not even that high. They are, however, beautiful and central so I had high hopes.

The original plan was to tackle them all in one day. By 'all', I will define what I classify as the 'Langdale Pikes' for the purposes of this book, as views differ on this. For me they are Loft Crag, Harrison Stickle, Pike O'Stickle, Pavey Ark, Sergeant Man, Thurnacar Knott and High Raise. Some only include the first three or the first four, as the others are not strictly part of the group. I wanted to cover them all, however. Off I set one morning in December as early as the light would allow. The weather forecast was for some mist but also patchy sunshine. Not perfect, but manageable. The ascent of Loft Crag from Dungeon Ghyll was lovely – varying terrains from grass to rock to marsh and to scrambles but a very pleasant climb. The only odd thing that happened was that as I was going up the mountain, two guys were coming down, one of whom was dripping blood from his face! I followed the blood drops up the rocky ascent for some way before it petered out – I began very early and they had got a long way up before me and got quite far back down again. There was no sign of camping equipment either. How early had they started and what had happened? I would love to know what the story behind that was. Anyway, I reached the top of Loft Crag at the same time as a thick mist came down. So, no views from Loft Crag then! Oh well, the forecasters said it would come and go so I decided to wait it out and have a coffee. So I did. And I waited. And waited. As it turned out, the forecasters were wrong! I had a map and compass but at this stage I was not using GPS and it was clear the mist was there to stay – and it was thick mist! So, I decided the safest option was to turn back and finish the Langdale Pikes another time. It can be soul-destroying to decide conditions are too poor to continue after you have done all the hard work to get there. It is often the sensible thing to do, however, and I would always advocate turning back if you are in any doubt.

So, phase two of climbing the Langdale Pikes took place the following holiday with my husband, Paul. This time, I went up the same way but bypassed Loft Crag to get straight to Pike O'Stickle with the aim of then taking in Thurnacar Knott, High Raise, Sergeant Man, Pavey Ark and end with Harrison Stickle and the route back to Dungeon Ghyll. At least, that was the theory... This time it was misty at the beginning but it cleared quite quickly to leave lovely views down the valley. We got to Pike O'Stickle but within three minutes the mist came down. Yes, the forecasters were wrong again, as this time it seemed there to stay. We decided to start the route to Thurnacar Knott in case things started to clear (this was a mistake as you will find out in Chapter Four: Bogs and Screes...). Things did not clear and after a quarter of a mile or so, I decided once again that safety needed to take priority and we made our way back down. I would probably have been braver with GPS.

Frankly, I was fed up with the route up from Dungeon Ghyll by then but, nonetheless, a couple of months later up I went, this time taking a variation on the previous route, towards Stickle Tarn to start at Harrison Stickle. The path up to Stickle Tarn has been repaired in

The Langdale Pikes.

Harrison Stickle.

recent years and there are rock steps a lot of the way up. The view at Stickle Tarn was simply stunning and worth every effort. The tarn was glistening in the sunlight and the forbidding rock massif of Pavey Ark stood behind as though guarding it. This is one of the most awe-inspiring views in the whole of Lakeland. Who would have thought somewhere so beautiful and rugged could exist for mere mortals to view? The way up to Harrison Stickle beckoned, however, so off I trekked, nose down, to the top. It was hard work but worth every step and there were plenty of beautiful views to sustain me in my high number of view stops. Finally getting to the top of a mountain I had walked past twice (via Pike O'Stickle and Loft Crag) gave me an even greater sense of achievement.

On I went to Pavey Ark – the first time I had managed to complete two in any one attempt! Real progress! But, alas, it was still not to be. I had been feeling increasingly unwell and for the third time, I made the decision that it would not be sensible to continue in case I got worse. My head was throbbing and I felt queasy and the heat and exertion were making it worse. Down once again to Dungeon Ghyll.

After that, I was on a mission. I would finish the Langdale Pikes if it killed me (chances are it would but there are worse ways to go). The final ascent began in Grasmere – I was going to do them with a bang! So, up Silver Howe from the Red Bank road, across to Blea Rigg then onto Sergeant Man, across to Thurnacar Knott and then High Raise. Silver How is a low fell but as the walk opened out onto bracken banks, the views started to appear and were wonderful down to Grasmere and along towards Rydal and Windermere. I do not say this often, but I reached the top of Silver How with fairly little effort – it seemed to be one of the only fells where the top is where you think it is. A wide rocky gully was the main part of the ascent and from there it was a mere skip to the summit cairn, delightful views of Loughrigg, Helm Crag and behind towards Blea Rigg, with part of the Langdales coming into sight. The sun was still shining so, filled with a sense of adventure and energy, I headed off towards Blea Rigg.

People have different views on their favourite ridge walks but the walk between Silver How and Blea Rigg, which is a series of little ups and downs with grassy hillocks and mini tarns, was lovely. It really was a stroll without any particular challenge until the final ascent and even that was gentle compared to most fells. From the summit of Blea Rigg, the view towards the Langdales opened up and included the sight of the rock massif of Pavey Ark. Sergeant Man beckoned, however.

The path to Sergeant Man from Blea Rigg is joined by the path from Stickle Tarn and a family of four were coming up that way. It is a popular route and for good reason as Stickle Tarn is beautiful. The family were studying their Wainwright book to find the route to Sergeant Man as the path was intermittent. This was all the navigation assistance they had – and it was the old Wainwright book at that, not the updated one. As I walked by them I became judgemental in my head about how silly it was to climb in the fells with only a Wainwright book – his books even say you need to have a good map with you as well at the very least. I, of course, had my Wainwright, my Ordnance Survey map and my GPS so was feeling all virtuous and experienced. Then, of course, I remembered my early fell-walking

Reflections on Easedale Tarn.

Easedale Tarn.

days and a climb up Brock Crags when I had not even been able to find my way out of the carpark with just a Wainwright (see Chapter Eight: Getting Lost! for more on that). I had done just the same when I started fell-climbing properly. We all learn.

So when I heard the family decide they should follow me as 'she looks like she knows where she is going' I had further flashbacks of the times I have done that and did not judge them anymore. Besides, I did know where I was going and it was the route they wanted, so they were in luck!

Sergeant Man was more of a challenge, as befits a higher fell and on the top of this one I knew I needed energy so had lunch. The sun was warm and shone on the surrounding fells like they were blessed. I certainly felt blessed to be there. It was busy from this point on as the Langdale Pikes are some of the most popular fells in the Lake District but I was in the mood for company so the cheery hellos and quick chats were very welcome.

I have to say that after the joy of the first three fells, Thurnacar Knott and High Raise lacked interest. There was very little ascent between them and the terrain was quite boggy and wet, with the summits quite dull. But to be honest, I was so pleased to be up there without mist it was hard to care! Done! At last! No hiccups, no problems, no mist! Where is the Dom Perignon when you need it? I needed a celebration! In the absence of Dom Perignon I had a 'Tigger moment' instead. This was a truly good moment. My day was not complete, however, as I had added Tarn Crag to the list for the day and off I went. I was quite tired by then, but still excited about the next fell.

The route from High Raise to Tarn Crag was tricky to find. There are no obvious paths and without my GPS I would probably still be looking for the route and the summit now. It was rather a meandering route, but the grass and heather and hillocks were all such deep and rich shades of green and the little bursts of pinks and yellows in some of the plants were really pretty. This is quite an unfrequented fell, particularly compared to the Langdale Pikes, which is a shame as it is an attractive fell with lumps and bumps everywhere and lots to look at. The summit just had a few rocks on the highest rock but the view down to Easedale Tarn and to Codale Tarn was beautiful and beyond towards Grasmere and Helm Crag – again, just lovely. I would absolutely recommend this fell to climb and I intend to climb it again as soon as I can.

I chose the route back to Grasmere via Easedale Tarn. This tarn was the first walk I ever did on my own and, therefore, holds fond memories for me. It is also very pretty and the last time I was there it was misty, so I was looking forward to seeing it in the sunshine. I was not disappointed and clearly I am not alone in that view as there were probably about 30 people in groups or couples enjoying the sunshine and the water. There were dinghies and canoes and people swimming and sunbathing. I stopped for a paddle (an intentional one, not falling in!) and then made my way down the path alongside Sour Milk Gill to Grasmere.

I had been walking for about seven hours over 12 miles and climbed over 3,000 feet/914 metres and had achieved my Langdale Pikes goal so – as my finances did not stretch to Dom Perignon – I had a shandy in Tweedies bar.

Steel Fell and Thirlmere Reservoir.

Never before in the history of the Lake District has one person taken so long and so many attempts to climb the Langdale Pikes. But I had done it at last!

Steel Fell to Gibson Knott – A cloud inversion!

Steel Fell is one I have wanted to climb for many years as I pass it so often on the way from Keswick to Grasmere and Ambleside. It has a very commanding presence as you approach it

from the Thirlmere side. Having studied my Wainwright guide and the OS map, I plotted a route on my GPS that would include Calf Crag and Gibson Knott as well. The weather was not promising with lots of low cloud (although a beautiful frost) but the weather people assured me it would improve during the day so off I set, starting from near the Swan Hotel at Grasmere. Grasmere is a beautiful village and has a rich heritage, not least the connection with William and Dorothy Wordsworth. It is surrounded by the central fells, including Helm

Steel Fell on a sunny afternoon.

Above the clouds.

Crag and is a good starting point for the Fairfield Horseshoe or towards the Langdale Pikes. There are some lovely cafés, restaurants and bars there as well, and the Jumble Room features in my favourite places in the Lake District.

The walk up Steel Fell was lovely – straightforward walking, a good path and easy gradients. I ended up in the cloud at one point so the views were poor, but about two-thirds of the way up I came out above the cloud. This is the first time that has happened to me – to be looking down on the cloud with a beautiful blue sky above but thick cloud below. I got a bit snap-happy with the camera at this point and have included the best ones here. Helm Crag looked amazing with the 'Howitzer' emerging from the mist. It really was a special sight.

From the summit of Steel Fell, the views down the Wythburn valley towards Thirlmere and across to Hellvelyn were excellent – just as they had promised to be from the road below. The route then headed towards Calf Crag. It was again an easy route with a good path for most of it. Or so I thought. As it turned out, I was so busy admiring the views and thinking how lucky I was to be out of the fells on such a great day that I was not paying attention to where I was putting my feet, thereby breaking a cardinal rule. I paid the price – one minute I was striding along, the next I was knee deep in a bog, plummeting forward... I saved myself from total submersion with a very un-elegant twist and turn onto my other leg and grabbing the heather on the other side of the bog. It must have been a sight to behold. I never knew I was such a gymnast – think I may have missed my calling...

I extracted myself from the bog, muttering about what on earth I was doing fell-walking in the mist and cold when I could be seeing the sights in Rome or Washington or somewhere. I was covered in bog but this is not a new experience for me, so once I had recovered my dignity, I brushed myself down and on I went. At this moment from the Far Easedale valley, a pack of hounds came charging up the fell – tails up, noses down and baying like souls in torment. Behind them came a farmer wearing a tweed jacket, tie, cap and leather boots. It was like something out of a fox-hunting scene in Sherlock Holmes. They were not hunting, just being exercised and it was quite a spectacle.

I made it to Calf Crag without further incident – although I admit I did stop and study the views when two men were coming the other way to ensure they saw my non-boggy side! As you know by now, I like to try and maintain some style when I am fell-walking, and whilst I do not always manage this, I see no reason to flaunt a boggy leg... (when I am exhausted from a walk I care less but this was a fairly easy one so I was still in caring mode).

Gibson Knott was the next fell on the route and this was a really nice walk with views into Far Easedale and beyond to Tarn Crag, High Raise and the Langdale Pikes. The weather held really well and I felt on top of the world. On the way down from Gibson Knott I met two Americans who had climbed over Helm Crag from Grasmere and were looking for the summit of Gibson Knott. The couple were on a two-week holiday from Washington State, near Seattle. I spent a few days in Seattle about five years ago – it is a great city. There is a famous mountain just outside the city called Mount Rainier – it is a popular destination for hiking and climbing (although I never ventured to its summit) but standing at over 14,400 feet/4,389 metres it is somewhat bigger than the Lake District Fells. I pointed the couple in the direction of the summit and said they were not far away. I noticed they were doing the walk using only a leaflet from the hotel they were staying at and it really did not give enough information. The part they were reading said they needed to head off Helm Crag towards Gibson Knott and then turn off left back towards Grasmere – it did not say they had to get to the summit of Gibson Knott so I thought they had walked too far. I explained to them using my OS map where they were and where I believed they should have turned back down to Grasmere (which was opposite the path I was going to take to get down into the opposite valley). I walked back with them to the crossroads of the path and set them on the right track and we chatted about Seattle. They were incredibly grateful and I hope they got back to the village without further problems.

My route took me down into the Greenburn Valley at Ghyll Foot and back towards the Swan Hotel. The amazing clouds from Steel Fell, the views across Far Easedale and opposite to the Hellvelyn Range meant this walk totally lived up to expectations. It is great when I drive along the road between Grasmere and Keswick now to know I have conquered Steel Fell and it is a route I would do again (watching where I put my feet!)

Fairfield Horseshoe – A windy winter wonderland

One of the most popular ridge walks in the Lake District must be the Fairfield Horseshoe. You can start it from some of the most popular locations (namely Grasmere and Ambleside) and with one or two minor exceptions, there are no technical difficulties. I have done this route twice – once in summer with my husband and more recently, in winter with snow and ice remaining on the higher fells. The fells climbed in this route are Nab Scar, Heron Pike, Great Rigg, Fairfield, Hart Crag, Dove Crag, High Pike and Low Pike.

The weather reports promised 'sunny intervals' so the Fairfield Horseshoe seemed like a good bet for a winter walk. I parked in the cricket carpark opposite Rydal Park. This is the closest I have been to anything cricket-related for many years, since I watched a match at Hove. I have no idea who was playing then, who won or whether the game was any good. I was there under sufferance. People cheered from time to time however so I suppose something interesting was happening. I love the idea of cricket and love the fact the village green is so close to my house and I can hear cricket being played in the summer. I even know the basic rules and the principles. I love the history of it and that it is so quintessentially English and I love it when the England team do well. But I just cannot get excited by watching it (I know, this will be heresy for some reading this and my head is duly hung in shame). However, a useful carpark with an honesty box for payment served a great purpose, so hurrah for cricket that day!

The walk through Rydal Park towards Rydal Hall was lovely – it is a gentle path that is a perfect warm-up for a long walk. However, as I arrived at the Rydal Hall estate, just getting up the steep driveway to the footpath was a bit challenging and I decided I must have overfilled my rucksack as it was feeling heavy already! I put this down to it being my first fell walk for nearly two months, however, and pressed on. The views started to open out over Windermere, Ambleside, Rydal Water and the fells beyond, so all thoughts of a heavy rucksack disappeared from my head. Amazingly, while the temperature at ground level was around 8 degrees, Rydal Water was still frozen and the ice formed amazing patterns, like the circles created by skimming stones.

It is quite steep in parts to Nab Scar but you feel quickly that you are making progress in height and there is a good path. At the top, the views towards Grasmere and Loughrigg and the Coniston Fells behind were impressive and I could see the fells of High Pike and Low Pike that would end the journey. My route took me next to Heron Pike, which is an odd name as it does not look like a pike and there are no herons apparent. It was a straightforward walk but from here onwards the signs of snow became more obvious on the ground and more care needed when walking. The continued straight walk to Great Rigg was also straightforward but at this point the wind increased dramatically. The snow was more abundant and as it was frozen rather than soft, it was even more precarious! As I reached the top of Great Rigg, it was all I could do to stay on my feet without being buffeted around.

For some reason I was finding the walk much more tiring than usual, yet I have climbed in deeper snow and been as cold. I have never walked in such strong winds (the tail end of Hurricane Katia on Hartsop Dodd and Wetherlam was but a mild breeze compared to this) but I was tired before it got windy so I could not put it down to that. My rucksack felt heavier than usual and on the top of Great Rigg I checked inside it in case I had left my hairdryer and heels in there. This is honestly true! I had put some of my creature

A sunny Fairfield Horseshoe.

comforts in the rucksack the night before to take down to the car to travel to the Lakes. A hairdryer and heels are not something I had intended to take up the mountain with me but I genuinely thought that as the bag was so heavy, I must have left them in there. I do not know how I would have missed them when packing the sandwiches, flask and water but in my head, this had to be the reason it was so heavy (I was cold so my thinking was clearly befuddled). Fortunately they were not there. If they had been, I would have donated the hairdryer to the next person I saw and taken the heels (hairdryers can be replaced, fabulous heels cannot!)

As I walked (or rather fought my way against the wind) towards Fairfield, it got colder and colder and I was looking forward to getting to the top and having a break. I finally made the summit and although the wind shelters were filled with snow, the wind had dropped and sitting against the wall on the outside was heavenly bliss! I reached into my rucksack (avoiding the lamps, curling irons and kitchen sink) and pulled out my sandwiches. I took my first bite and they were frozen! All that effort and such anticipation and they were inedible! At that moment I could have cried! A large crow (who cared nothing for my distress) was looking at me pleadingly and so I gave in and threw him a sandwich. He

Skimming stones on a frozen Rydal Water.

A domestic goddess?

looked well pleased! When I threw him the other one as well, he thought his birthday and Christmas had come at once and managed to fit them both in his beak and flew off low over the fell to take the rest of the day off from hunting! I, on the other hand, made do with coffee and a cereal bar!

Once recovered, I took a moment to soak up the views. The 'sunny intervals' had not materialised but despite that, the surrounding fells that were close were not in cloud and I could see St Sunday Crag and across to the Red Screes. The sky may not have been blue, but the snow made the scene fascinating with the wind blowing it into glossy drifts on the edges of some mountains like glossy meringues (glossier than the ones I make anyway) but leaving earthy stripes on others.

As I was about to leave Fairfield, a lone guy came up from the same route I had taken. He had no rucksack, no map and no GPS. He asked me what way he needed to go to do the rest of the horseshoe, how far it was and how long it would take. I told him and off he set like he was out for a Sunday afternoon stroll in the summer rather than a hard slog in the cold winter. This is not a sensible way to travel in the fells and I would not recommend it ever (anyone can get into difficulties and you need to be prepared for everything). I confess I felt slightly envious of his care-free approach and I was almost tempted to ask him to carry my rucksack back down for me!

I braced myself for the second half of the horseshoe, happy in the knowledge I had done most of the hard work. The walk over Hart Crag and Dove Crag was lovely and the views in both valleys were superb. The crags between the two mountains could be seen at close range and were striking. The snow was still quite deep but the wind was much less and although I was tired, I knew I was on the home stretch. That said, it is still a long way! High Pike was completed and then it was onto Low Pike – the final fell of the day. As I came over Low Pike, a ray of sunshine appeared. Ah! One of those 'sunny intervals' at last! At least I think it was a ray of sunshine, it was so fleeting that it could have been the glint from the eye of a very well-fed crow....

Looking back to Heron Pike and Great Rigg gave me a real spur to think I had come so far. Low Pike sounds like it should be a doddle, but beware of complacency. On the path down from Low Pike is an enormous rock step that makes the 'Bad Step' on Crinkle Crags look easy. I remembered encountering it the first time on the Horseshoe in the summer and I needed help to get down – despite my height and long legs – so when I came upon it this time, I opted for the easier option of walking the longer route around. However, the obvious path leads right to the step so it is a case of retracing your steps if you come across it.

I was near the end now and I had plotted a route that would take me right back to the carpark and not into Ambleside, as that would have added probably another mile to the journey (which my feet would have protested about most strongly!) My GPS was now telling me, however, that I was heading into Ambleside and I needed to be further to the right. So I hot-footed it up the field to a rather large wall. As I stood on tiptoe and peered over the top, I could see my car in the cricket carpark in the distance. Hurrah! There was only one problem – the wall was higher than me. I had no intention of letting it beat me, however, and whilst getting over it was inelegant, it was effective.

The car was a welcome sight and I headed back towards Grasmere for a well-earned hot chocolate and contemplation of my achievement of 11 miles and over 3,000 feet/914 metres of ascent. I was tired but happy (although still puzzled about the weight of the rucksack – it really must have been that I was not very fit!)

Rosthwaite Fell to Rosset Pike – sometimes it isn't about the views!

I was very excited about this walk – I had planned it for months and according to the weather forecast, there should have been sunny spells the day I did it. Probably needless to say, those 'sunny spells' did not materialise until we were on the route to the final fell. There were no views until that moment but I loved it nevertheless and it incorporated Bessyboot (Rosthwaite Fell), Glaramara, Allen Crags, Esk Pike, Bowfell and Rosset Pike – starting at Stonethwaite and ending in Great Langdale. Totalling 15 miles and 4,600 feet/1,402 metres of ascent, this was the longest and highest climb I had done.

My husband Paul was unlucky enough to be with me on this walk. His love of fell-walking is limited at the best of times – it does not help that he injured his ankle playing football when he was younger and sometimes it still causes problems. However, he perseveres and I am the designated driver each holiday so he can sample the local bitters – this compromise seems to work well.

Earthy Stripes.

Leaving the car at Stonethwaite, we headed on the path used on a previous walk that heads towards Eagle Crag but branches up to the right quite early on to start the ascent of Bessyboot. The initial ascent is steep and looks like work has been done on the steps to repair them. You follow a river with cascades, which is beautiful. As the first third of the ascent is in a wood, the green mosses are in full force and there is a damp feel; it is eerie and lovely. At least it was until I was having a break and whilst asking my husband what the strange decomposing smell was, noticed a dead sheep just behind me. It frightened the life out of me and was horrible to see. I do not know how it had met its fate but it was not in the last couple of days. Poor thing.

It was an incentive to end the rest stop though and after another 10 minutes, we emerged from the wood. After a bit of a scramble over a rocky/broken wall area, we found ourselves in more marshy territory, with a range of streams and water outlets and a series of little ups

and downs heading towards the main summit. Bessyboot is not the true summit of the fell but it is the popular interpretation. It is actually part of the Rosthwaite Fell and the summit of that is higher and further along the path. We headed towards the Rosthwaite summit and Rosthwaite Cam, an enormous rocky part of Rosthwaite Fell that would be in good company with the Bowder Stone!

The next fell was Glaramara. In Book IV of his 'Pictorial Guide to the Lakeland Fells' series 'The Southern Fells', Wainwright says of the route between Bessyboot and Glaramara that 'a path would improve matters' (Rosthwaite Fell 5) and should be avoided in mist. This did not bode well as it was very misty. I was confident in my GPS, however, and knew we would find the summit. Well, we did find it. However, at one point, when we had been following a quite distinctive path, I looked at the GPS and it said we were too far to the left. I had not seen an alternative path though and had been looking carefully. At that point, the mist

Glaramara – on a rather sunnier day!

cleared for a brief second and I could see we were at right angles to where we should have been with a valley in front and a mountain range beyond. That was wrong. We should have a valley on our left not in front. Glaramara and an increase in height was supposed to be in front! We therefore made our own path to get back in line with the GPS, which took about 15 minutes and then used it as a constant guide to ensure we did not stray from the 'path' again. It is amazing how quickly we went wrong and how we nearly ended up in a totally different valley, but for the magic of GPS. It was an unconventional route to the summit of Glaramara but we made it at last, although it was extremely tiring on the slopes away from a proper path. Without GPS it is a test I would have failed, as many others have done before me.

Whilst there were no views on Glaramara, it was a great summit – very rocky and interesting. (It is such a pretty name as well that it inspired me to research what it meant when I got back down.) At this point, Paul was starting to flag and as it was only fell number two of six, we pressed on. The next fell was Allen Crags. This at least was a straightforward path from one to the other and I imagine on a better day has wonderful views. One thing we did see however was a very pretty little tarn in a rocky setting – 'a perfect mountain tarn' according to Wainwright and he may be right again (Allen Crags 7 of 'The Southern Fells').

A longer rest on Allen Crags was in order with coffee and sandwiches. For brief fleeting moments, the clouds would move and we had a feel for what the views would be like. I am keen to do this walk again for that reason. Esk Pike beckoned and again, the path was straightforward to Esk Hause, which is a major crossroads for people walking towards Scafell Pike or for those heading into Borrowdale or the opposite valley, Langdale. At this point having seen no one for several hours, it was suddenly a busy highway. The mist was thick, the rain was soft but relentless, still there were no views and having seen no one for several hours, it was suddenly a busy highway.

Our route took us off to the left but as I mentioned earlier on in the book, this was a real test of technology over instinct. There did not seem to be an obvious path so we headed off in the direction we believed Esk Pike to be in (bearing in mind we could see nothing). I kept checking the GPS, however, and it said we needed to be heading pretty much at a right-angle to where we were. We headed in the direction it highlighted and both of us thought we were walking back on ourselves towards Allen Crags. We stopped and discussed what was best to do – our instincts were telling us we were going the wrong way but the GPS said it was right. I thought it best to do what the GPS said at least for a short distance. Paul agreed (he usually leaves the route planning and map reading to me as I love all that and he does not) so we followed the highlighted route. After about five minutes we started heading upwards on an obvious path. It was definitely not the path we had come down for Allen Crags so it must be Esk Pike. Hurrah for GPS – on the technology versus instinct battle, GPS won.

It was a rocky but exhilarating climb to Esk Pike. On reaching that summit (still no views) I started to feel like we were making real progress and was enjoying it no end. Paul, on the other hand, was finding the lack of views a problem and the 'I could be on a beach in Barbados' look was starting to appear in his eyes, so I avoided catching his eye but started a positive conversation about how we had done most of the hard work and it would not be long before we were in a pub having a beer. Sadly, he stopped being fooled by that a long time ago and I suspect my positive optimism was more irritating than helpful. Silence can be golden sometimes, so I shut up and we moved off Esk Pike down to Ore Gap.

Occasionally through the mist, when we had got to Ore Gap, the dark, looming mass of Bowfell appeared as a forbidding shadow. It did not look tempting in this weather, but as we had come so far I was determined to do it. Having said Esk Pike was rocky, Bowfell was a boulder graveyard that got more and more of a scramble the closer to the top you got. It was a great climb though and the summit surprised me. For some reason, I had expected a large summit with rocks, of course, but extensive and mainly flat. It is not like that at all. The cairn is tiny and perched on top of the highest boulder and the summit itself is small. My previous attempt at Bowfell had been cut short at Three Tarns owing to a wrong turn (pre-GPS) that meant I did Pike O'Blisco rather than Crinkle Crags (see Chapter Eight: Getting Lost! for that shameful story), so by the time I had done Crinkle Crags as well, I was too tired to continue to Bowfell.

I closed my eyes at the cairn and tried to imagine what I should have seen from there had the mist decided to clear. I had seen the various valleys from other fells on other occasions, so had some idea but it was hard to do and really of little consolation at the time. Anyway, there was only one fell left, so we headed back down to Ore Gap, which like Esk Hause was suddenly very busy despite the weather, and then headed onto Angle Tarn. It was here that the sun finally emerged and the mist started to clear. The views of the crags, rocks and cliffs of Bowfell were amazing from Angle Tarn and the Tarn itself was beautiful. I was pleased that we had at last got something to see.

Having walked so far and climbed so high in the last few hours, Rosset Pike proved a challenge for tired legs. It is a great little fell (although perhaps I am biased as it was the only one we had views from that day). The long route down to Langdale was via Rosset Gill and although long, it was a fabulous walk with the Gill always nearby.

My mum and dad were picking us up from near the National Trust carpark and I had originally given them a time of 4pm. Oh, such an optimist! The detour between Bessyboot and Glaramara had added at least half an hour to the journey and I had underestimated the overall time. The fact I was not on my own also usually means it takes longer as you chat more and debate routes for longer. My last update when I had a mobile phone signal gave a revised time of 5pm to mum and dad. As our tired legs reached the car, however, it was nearer 6pm and I could tell that as well as looking up at the fell to see any sign of us, they had also been looking for any sign of the Mountain Rescue helicopter in case one of us had fallen. They had tried to remind themselves that we were sensible walkers and would not take risks, but I felt very bad about being so late and I am much more careful with my walking times now when I am getting a lift.

They took us back to Stonethwaite. Paul and I had a drink in the Langstrath pub (Paul had a smile on his face for the first time since Allen Crags) and then we all met up again that evening in Bassenthwaite for dinner. It was a hard walk and the weather was only kind in the closing stages, but I just love the exhilaration and sense of achievement whether or not I can see any views. Of course I prefer beautiful sunny and warm or cold and crisp days for walking, but there is something about the Lake District that captures me and I felt like I had met the challenge that day. Fantastic.

Note: Glaramara comes from Old Norse and means the 'mountain with a shieling (mountain hut) by a ravine'. This is less romantic than I had hoped, sadly!

The Coniston Range – Don't forget the suncream!

Probably one of the most popular and well-known mountains in the Lake District is the Old Man of Coniston (or Coniston Old Man). Coniston is also a pretty and popular village. Coniston Water is also beautiful and famous for its connection with Donald Campbell, who attempted to break his own water speed record on Coniston in 1967 in the Bluebird K7 and sadly lost his life in the process (his body was not found until 2001). The Old Man of Coniston also features in Arthur Ransome's 'Swallows and Amazons' (1930) as 'Kanchenjunga'. The summit of The Old Man of Coniston is, therefore, usually a busy place. The rest of the Coniston range, however, is slightly less frequented. It is well worth a visit for the spectacular views and for the fact that once you are on the ridge, you can stroll along it for miles on good paths, without any particular hardship.

I remember climbing The Old Man of Coniston when I was young with my dad and brother. From memory, we went up the popular tourist route starting from the carpark at the top of the no through road from Coniston village. In 2009, however, I climbed the whole range with my husband Paul in the most glorious sunshine! Sun cream was applied with gusto! This time, the route began from the top of the Wrynose Pass at the Three Shire Stone and the first fell was Grey Friar up the Wet Side Edge path, which was an ascent of 1,350 feet/411 metres over two and a quarter miles. To be clear, Wet Side Edge was dry with a good path. It was steep towards the top before gaining the ridge, but each step upwards gave ever more amazing views behind over Pike O'Blisco, Cold Pike and Crinkle Crags, so there was always a good reason for a view stop! We kept to the right across the dip called 'Fairfield' (not to be confused with the fell Fairfield) and headed up the last stretch to Grey Friar on a grassy path.

I did not really know a lot about Grey Friar before climbing it. It is probably one of the less frequented fells in the Coniston range as it is slightly out on a limb from the main ridge, but I have to say it is probably my favourite of that area. The summit is rather a rock graveyard but is all the more interesting for that with plenty of grass in between for comfortable walking. More importantly, however, the views were outstanding. A beautiful seascape to the left first captures the eye and as you sweep to the right, you can see the whole of the Scafell range in all its majesty about five miles away. You can also see the Skiddaw range, Blencathra and much of the Hellvelyn range, along with parts of the Fairfield Horseshoe and, of course, the closer Coniston fells. Wonderful!

Dragging ourselves away from the Grey Friar summit we headed towards Great Carrs, which was a grassy stroll and only a short climb. The summit brought in some of the fells in the east of the Lake District, including much of the High Street range and Red Screes. You can also see down to Windermere and Elterwater and across the Wrynose Pass to the Red Tarn between Pike O'Bisco and Crinkle Crags. An unusual addition to this summit is the presence of wreckage from an aeroplane that did not quite clear the mountain back in World War II. Much of this wreckage was taken down to the Ruskin museum in Coniston in 1997, but some remains on the summit and as you walk to Swirl How, you can see some of the wreckage on the scree slope below.

The next stop was Swirl How, which is less than half a mile away. The summit cairn is perched on the edge of a steep drop. Coniston Water comes into view for the first time from this summit and on a clear day you can see the Isle of Man, as we could on that day.

We had seen maybe five or six people on the route so far but looking ahead towards Coniston Old Man, it was already possible to see how busy that summit was! Our next stop though was Brim Fell, which again was an easy walk without any challenge of note. The most striking view on the route was the Levers Water, which for me was seen at its best from the dip at Levers Hawse. The water was a striking blue and the obvious pale cream paths surrounding it made a beautiful contrast. If we had not had such a long route planned that day, I would have loved to have walked down to it. It was a very beautiful scene.

Clouds and shadows from Grey Friar.

Low Water.

As a summit, Brim Fell itself lacks interest as it is merely a large grassy dome. However, the whole, almost straight route from Great Carrs to Coniston Old Man was proving such a joy with such stunning views that I could easily forgive it for having rather a dull summit! The route to the Old Man was easy with barely any ascent (about 30 metres towards the large cairn) and there were a huge number of people. Some find hoards of people on fell tops annoying as they crave solitude. I have some sympathy with that view as it is nice to be on your own or with a friend/family member and enjoy the quiet and scenery. However, the Lake District is so beautiful that I also think it is wonderful to see so many people enjoying it and getting up onto the fells. The range of people on the top of Coniston Old Man was fantastic: young and old, large groups to individuals, people who were clearly regular fell walkers and those who were probably climbing their first fell. At that moment, however, we all had one thing in common. We were all looking with either quiet or exuberant joy at the views from Coniston to the surrounding fells and from the sea to the Pennines, and we all had a sense of achievement for having reached the summit.

What is less apparent from the top, but clear on the routes up Coniston Old Man from the valley, are the scars of human activity on that fell and its neighbours. In the past, copper mining was predominant on the fell and whilst that has now ceased, many of the old mine workings remain with tunnels and shafts, particularly in an area known as Coppermines Valley. The dangerous shafts are fenced off but do take care if you explore the area. Whilst the mining of copper has ended, quarrying remains part of the industrial activity on the fell.

So that was the ridge route from Grey Friar to Old Man of Coniston. Or so you would think! Sadly for my legs but happily for my eyes, we had to take the whole route back to the Wrynose Pass to get back to the car! I had not broken this news to Paul at the beginning of the route so he looked less than pleased with me, but had to admit that he was enjoying the walk so off we set back the way we had come. Dow Crag on the left as we returned was a striking backdrop and a fell I had yet to climb, but I did not think now was the time to suggest a detour! We avoided the actual summits on the way back and tried to keep at a consistent level to avoid unnecessary ascent and it did not take too long before Great Carrs was back under our feet. We took the Wet Side Edge route down again back to the car – we were very tired but very content with life!

At this point, I should highlight the importance of sun cream when you are walking in the fells in the summer (or indeed spring and autumn if you are lucky enough to find warm sunshine). I burn quite easily so always keep applying sun cream and wear a hat as well. The higher the factor the better as you do not want to end up with stripes when you are wearing shorts and walking socks. I will not say who that happened to on this walk (but it was not me...).

The Coniston range was a fantastic walk. Those with lots of energy can take in Wetherlam and Dow Crag as well if they choose to and can also explore the coppermines. Once you are up on the main ridge, it is a joy to stroll between the fells.

I hope these ridge walks have given a flavour of some of the different areas of fell walking in the Lake District. Other routes I have done include:

■ Hellvelyn Range from Dollywagon Pike to Clough Head (10 mountains, over 12 miles and 4,000 feet/1,219 metres of ascent) – not for the faint of foot!

■ Raven Crag to Bleaberry Fell (via Armboth, High Tove and High Seat) from the Thirlmere dam – watch out for the bogs! Best done on a frosty day...

■ Cauldale Moor to Yoke (via Thornthwaite Crag, Froswick and Ill Bell) from the top of the Kirkstone Pass – a joyous ridge walk but watch out for the steep bit to Thornthwaite!

■ Carrock Fell to Great Calva (via High Pike and Knott) from Stone Ends Farm – one for those who are craving solitude.

■ Bowscale to Souther Fell (via Bannerdale Crags and Mungrisdale Common) from Mungrisedale – take my advice and avoid Mungrisdale Common (see Chapter Two: Divided by a Common Language, to see why)!

There are many others and half the fun is plotting your own routes among the fells as the variations and options are numerous.

Chapter Four: Bogs and Screes (and a wet river crossing!)

Sometimes, just climbing a mountain is not exciting enough (?) and adding an extra challenge gives it a little frisson! I have to confess, however, that the extra challenges are not always planned...

Boggy adventures (or 'Thank goodness I was not wearing Jimmy Choos!')

I have a natural affinity with bogs. I wish I did not but I do. I put it down to my overly optimistic nature. I always think it cannot be that deep, or if I take one step on that marsh

Beware of bogs!

plant it will give me momentum to get to the other side, or I think I can stretch my legs further than I can. That is one part of it. The other is that sometimes, I am so swept up in the views that I just do not look where I am putting my feet. So while it pains me to do it given my aspiration to retain style even when climbing fells, I felt I should include something about bogs so you can all benefit from my experience (not something I have put on my CV) and help you avoid my errors!

Many of you will know that the fells can be very boggy – particularly in wet weather – and some mountains are renowned for peat bogs, marshy bogs or various other types of bogs. (Here, I confess my knowledge on types of bogs is poor and I have no intention of changing that – they are all wet and muddy and that is all I need to know.) Some are worse than others, however, and places like Armboth Fell and the ridge walk from there across High Tove, High Seat and Bleaberry Fell should be avoided at all costs in my view if you are not a bog fan. (Actually, it is better to do that route when there is a frost on the ground as they are boggy even in a dry summer and the frost keeps things bearable.)

At the beginning of a walk, I always try and avoid puddles and mud and try to keep my boots clean (no comment). After a few miles or a few thousand feet of ascent, however, I am less fussy, and therefore more prone to stumble across (and into!) a bog. The first time this happened was on the Langdale Pikes between Pike O'Stickle and Thurnacar Knott. I was walking merrily away when all of a sudden, my right leg disappeared beneath me and my left leg stumbled forward so my knee disappeared the same way! I was well and truly in a bog! Now, those who have never been in a bog (highly sensible and commendable but do not crow too loudly as you never know) may find it hard to imagine, but it was a real shock and I immediately felt myself being sucked further in.

When I was little, I watched the Jeremy Brett version of Sherlock Holmes's 'The Hound of the Baskervilles'. At the end, the bad guy strikes out across the Devon moors and gets lost. He gets stuck in a bog and slowly gets sucked down into it and drowns! Well – that was my first thought! I was going to be sucked right in! Absolutely no way in the world, though, was it going to say on my gravestone that I had been killed in a bog! I would not end my days here on this mountain in this bog. So I gripped the heather around the edge and with enormous conviction, pulled my left knee out and then got a stronger grip to extract my right leg. I then lay exhausted and boggy on the edge. Not a good look. I had to get through the rest of the excursion in that condition until I found a stream. I will let you use your imagination about the reaction of my husband. Let's just say I imagine the laughter was heard in the valley below (and he has never fallen in a bog – life is unfair!).

Since then, it has become a rather too-familiar scene and I have stepped in bogs on Gibson Knott, Tarn Crag (Long Sleddale) and Bleaberry Fell, to name but a few. It even happened recently when walking through the fields to Tunbridge Wells! It is quite a family talking point (sigh…).

Screes

Another fell-walking banana skin to be aware of is screes. I am always up for a challenge and when I read the maps, guide books and Wainwright's before a fell walk, I try and choose an ascent/descent or a ridge route that will give a different perspective, type of climb or challenge before I decide the route. It is not always the longest or the shortest or the steepest or gentlest. I have learned a few lessons over my time as this book is starting to show, but I had yet to learn the lesson of screes. Screes are basically areas of loose shattered rock or slate of some description. They are difficult to walk on and it is easy to slip because the rocks are just piled on top of each other and are very unstable.

The Grasmoor Screes – Pay attention to contours!

One such route was when I tackled Grasmoor. This is a fell I had wanted to climb for several years – it has that 'come and climb me' challenge about it and every time I was in the Buttermere and Crummock area, it was Grasmoor that captured my attention (and trust me, after this experience it always will!). I read everything I could about the fell and decided I would tackle the scree route. I had never done anything like that before so it would be a new experience. Well, that was about the only thing I was right about. According to the Wainwright guide the climb is 2,430 feet/740 metres over one and a quarter miles. It sounded steep but hey, if Wainwright had managed it, then I was sure I could.

The Grasmoor Screes – avoid!

Snowy Dore Head Scree.

It was June 2010 and a beautiful sunny day with hardly a cloud in the sky. I pulled into the carpark near Rannerdale and looked up at the scree. It did look pretty daunting. In his guide book, Wainwright says:

'It needs an experienced eye fully to appreciate from the foot of the slope the length of the scree run in Red Gill. Most observers will seriously underestimate both its length and steepness.'

(Book 6 "The Northwestern Fells" page Grasmoor 7)

This should have set my alarm bells ringing immediately, as should the fact that the scree route did not appear in the other guide books I had read. However, off I went across the grass to the foot of the fell. And looked up. And up. And up. Golly it was steep! I started upwards. Onwards I went and completed the grassy slope without any difficulties. At that point I looked back towards the carpark (which you can see the whole way up) and started

to worry about whether I had locked the car (ever had that feeling?). There was no way at this point I was going back though! They were welcome to my Madonna CDs. I admired the view instead across Crummock Water to Mellbreak and across to the High Stile Range. Stunning. I started the scree.

It was fine for the first third – steep but there were black sacks full of rocks for the Fix the Fells teams to repair the scree and I used those as milestones between view stops. Then the black sacks ran out and the scree got steeper. And then steeper again. By the two-thirds point, it splits into two distinctive tongues. Wainwright says to use the one on the left. To me though, the one on the right looked less steep so I ploughed on that way. Mistake. At various points, I was clinging onto dry pieces of earth at the edge of the scree feeling like I was nearly vertical and that if I let go, I would fall. On the rare occasions I had the nerve to look down, I actually felt in danger from the steepness and that if I slipped, I would be in serious trouble. It was exhausting, with every step being no more than a few inches and then many steps slipping back again as I tried to grip. The sun, which had been so beautiful to me as I started, was now a torment without shade and it felt like 100 degrees C. For the first time ever I wanted to turn around and go back, but that looked even more dangerous so was not an option! I had to go onwards and upwards. Sometimes, I took a step and felt I was falling: there was nothing to hold onto... my trousers and sleeves and hands were covered in dust and mud. I was tired and, if I am honest, a little scared.

Why on earth had I chosen this route? Why did I not listen to the alarm bells? Why did I choose the right-hand scree tongue and not the left one as Wainwright said? Why did I want to be climbing mountains anyway? I would rather do Striding Edge a dozen times than be where I was.

It took me about an hour and a half to do the final third of the scree. I think I was the most exhausted I have ever been. Eventually, the scree ended, the heather increased and the slope became more gentle. Each step at that point was a step in heaven as far as I was concerned. Just to be off the scree was bliss. I cannot explain the relief. I finally got to the cairn – I was a dusty, muddy and tired sight to behold and never has a cairn looked more beautiful. I collapsed in the wind shelter. There was a man there drinking coffee and he kept glancing at me. After a while, he turned properly to look at me and said 'Did you come up Grasmoor Edge?' I turned my tired head towards him and said 'No, I came up the scree.' 'Dear me, lass! You should be on the telly!' he replied. You know what? After that effort I agreed with him! (Clearly the hair and make-up department would have a job to do first as I could not possibly look how I did!)

When I had recovered, I went back to the car via Whiteless Pike (it is surprising how quickly you recover when the summit is reached even after that level of exertion). Absolutely never again though... I would never recommend doing Grasmoor that way. I do look back and feel a sense of enormous achievement and I am proud that I conquered all the fear and kept going. Each time I am in the Crummock area I always park in the Rannerdale carpark, look up at the scree and remember. It takes an experienced eye to appreciate the steepness and length of the scree run on Grasmoor, you know – I now have that experience!

More screes

Just when you think I would have learned my lesson about screes, I decided to do the Mosedale Horseshoe from Wasdale Head and finish by coming down the Dore Head screes between Red Pike and Yewbarrow. I have covered that walk in more detail in Chapter Five as one of the fells that day was Steeple, which I love. Apparently there is a nice grassy, albeit steep, path next to the Dore Head screes, but I never found it and ended up climbing (or rather slipping) down the screes themselves. It was not a pretty sight, was very tiring, very dusty and not at all elegant. It turns out that going down screes is no better than climbing up them!

Since then I have found myself on several smaller scree areas around Carrock Fell, Mellbreak, Silver Howe and others but, none of them were particularly long or steep. This

Cross with great care.

is a deliberate choice as, while I am actually quite good at walking on scree and do not mind a short stretch, I do not enjoy the feeling of terrain so loose that I cannot control my feet. Screes are dangerous. When I climbed Kirk Fell in December 2011, I had been planning to go the direct route up. However, as I was about to start the route, I could see the scree section at the top was covered in snow and I decided to be sensible and take the longer route to the top. At last I am trying to pay attention to the lessons I have learned.

A wet river-crossing!

If I have to cross a river by hopping across rocks I always check to see no one is around before I start in case a hop from rock to rock turns into a hop from rock to splash! I have avoided this catastrophe on most occasions, but one time I was not so lucky was descending Lank Rigg.

As I approached the crossing of River Calder I could see it was flowing high and fast following all the recent rain. Apparently, you can usually use the stones to get across. They looked a little dodgy to me though – slippery and wet with several of them underwater, and the rapids were quite fast. It looked quite deep as well. I walked down the river a little to see if there was a better place and then up it, but to no avail. This was the only place to cross. I was not feeling positive about it. However, I had to get across it so I put my best foot forward and placed a foot tentatively on the first rock. Great – it was fine. I placed my other foot on the next likely-looking rock and then the one after that. So far, so good. It was not as hard as I thought!

Restoring dignity away from bogs and screes.

My next step was not to be. As soon as I put any weight on it, my boot slipped off the rock and landed in the water, I swung my arms around valiantly trying to balance (I dread to think what I looked like) and for a brief moment, I thought I had saved myself with only a wet foot. Then over I went – plunging backwards straight into the water, catching myself with both hands so I was effectively sitting in the river. Mortifying! All dignity and style gone. I leapt up as I was worried about the rucksack getting wet but it was all that was keeping me afloat as it turned out. I missed my footing again and plunged back down into the water, travelling forward about three or four metres as I was pushed by the current of the river and ended up wedged between two rocks. An abject picture of misery. Poor me!

I must have been sitting in the water for at least 30 seconds before I had the wherewithal to drag myself up and onto the bank. A sad, drenched person with probably a dozen fish in my boots. I felt so miserable that I did not even care if anyone had seen me (which is a first for me in this type of situation). However, I do have a sense of humour and, while I cannot always laugh at myself straight away, I usually pull myself together quickly. And I did. I could feel a tingle of laughter coming over me and the more I thought about the incident, how I must have looked and how I had nearly got swept away in the raging torrents of the deep forbidding river (well, that's how it would be when I described it, not just this little stream with a few inches of water), the more I laughed. So I went from a picture of abject misery to a picture of deranged maniacal laughter!

I got myself up and squelched my way along the remaining two miles of path back to the car and then drove all the way to Coniston for a well-deserved hot chocolate in the Bluebird Café.

Note to self – next time I am faced with a dodgy river crossing, I will take my boots off and walk across avoiding the rocks. Far better to have wet feet and a little dignity than be soaked through with no dignity.

I am not sure my husband would have appreciated knowing someone so wet was getting in his car but it could have been worse – after all, it could have been my car!

Chapter Five: My Favourite Fells (Part I)

This is a tricky one for me as my favourite mountains depend on a range of factors. For some, it is because I love the ascent or the particular terrain, for others it is the ridge walk. Even the mood or place in my life I was at when I climbed a fell impacts sometimes. Then of course, there are the views, about which I could write enough to rival the length of 'War and Peace' given a free rein.

In this chapter and Chapter Seven, I have tried to capture my favourite individual mountains and the reasons why I love them. They are not necessarily the highest, the most famous or the most popular mountains but I love them. People reading this book will agree with some and think I am crazy about others as it is all about personal choice. I am always interested to hear what fells people enjoy climbing and why.

Yewbarrow – my favourite mountain.

Yewbarrow

If push came to shove, I think I would have to name Yewbarrow as my absolute favourite fell. It would be a close-run thing with Mellbreak, but Yewbarrow has the advantage of being in my favourite area in the Lake District, Wasdale and overlooks my favourite lake, Wastwater. You also have stunning views over the Scafells, Great Gable, Pillar, the Wastwater Screes of Illgill Head and Win Rigg and even out to sea. My climb of Yewbarrow in January 2011 was also at rather a career crossroads in my life and the magic of it helped me take a completely different direction (hence this book) and I have not looked back since.

It was a beautiful cold, sunny day with barely a cloud in the bright blue sky and, as I drove along the road past Wastwater and admired the eerie screes, I felt a real sense of excitement for the climb ahead. A perfect day. It does not matter how often I see the screes, they always make me draw breath when they first come into sight as they are so imposing and mystical.

I parked at Overbeck Bridge and looked up at Yewbarrow – Bell Rib (the large rocky outcrop near the top) looked daunting and imposing but exciting. I locked the car and started to walk towards the path, GPS in hand. Then I went back to the car as I had forgotten my hat. Off I went again. Two minutes later I was heading back to the car as I had forgotten my gloves. Right – I was definitely off this time! I went through the gate and up the path to the first ridge where I took my first view stop (about five minutes from the car). I often wonder in the early stages of the climb how I am ever going to get to the top. Although I am pretty fit, I still get out of breath and have to stop often! My walking style is to go in short, fast spurts and then stop. I am not a plodder that keeps going. The advantage of frequent stops is remembering to keep looking behind and around at the view and not just ahead. Each stop I took on the grassy slope had ever more amazing views of Wastwater, the screes and the surrounding mountains. I did my usual trick of choosing milestones up the long slope until I reached the stony path towards Bell Rib.

Stony/rocky paths are my best walking terrain – I am a much better walker on those types of surfaces than grassy ones, where my legs feel more drained by the soft earth. This path, however, was very steep but I persevered and each step took me closer to my destination and showed me even more inspiring views. It was a case of legs and hands for much of the ascent at this point – but part of the joy of climbing for me is scrambling as it takes my mind off how steep it is and feels like an adventure. I kept an eye on my GPS, but for a while it had not moved and it looked like I was still in the same place on the map. 'Ah!' I thought, 'the batteries must have gone!' So I sat down and got two rechargeable batteries out of my rucksack (rechargeable batteries are the most cost-effective way to power a GPS device in my opinion, especially if you look at it as much as I do!) After I had changed the batteries I climbed a bit further and looked at the GPS again – but it still looked like I had not moved. Very odd! And then it dawned on me... the path was so steep, that from a satellite perspective, I was almost vertical and therefore making very little forward progress! It was honestly that steep!

The path takes you to the left of the Bell Rib rock face that you can see for most of the route up and when you are almost parallel with the top of it, you realise it really is a long way from the top of the fell! Once again, what looked like the top had fooled me! I was really enjoying the climb though and when the path split and became unclear, I decided to keep to the right hand side as I hoped that this would be where the best views to Wastwater would be. At one point, there was a narrow rock corridor called Great Door and I was not sure if I could fit through it (rucksack being too large of course, not me, clearly!) On balance though I thought I could probably fit so I began the climb up the gully. However, as I got to the top of the corridor it looked as though if I went much further I would be stepping into oblivion, so I decided to retreat and scramble up the left-hand side of the gully instead. When I appeared on the top of the ridge, I looked down to where I would have come and I was right – there was a sheer drop. Good decision to retreat!

Once the shock of that had gone, I looked out from the ridge to the views around. There really is not a word that can describe that view: 'breathtaking' and 'magical' are about as close as it gets, but even that cannot convey the overwhelming sense of wellbeing and inner happiness I felt at that moment. I could look at that view forever and be perfectly content. The sun glinted and winked on the still water of Wastwater and the frost that remained on some of the higher fells looked like someone had sprinkled diamonds on them (if that had been true I would have abandoned Yewbarrow and headed straight for them, obviously!)

However, I still had to get to the top, so I followed the ridge for about half a mile. It was one of the finest ridge walks I have ever done, with the views to Great Gable, Kirk Fell and Pillar opening up beyond to join the already amazing views of the Scafells, screes and in the opposite direction, Middle Fell and Haycock. Reaching the top was one of the most amazing feelings and I had such a sense of achievement. I walked to the other end of the top, however, as that part of the fell was in sunshine. I sat on the rocks without seeing another soul and even though it was January, it felt warm in the sunshine. It was at this point, feeling this euphoric, that I made a life-changing career decision (hence this book and my blog). Such was the magic of Yewbarrow.

I had to deal with a small part of reality, however, as before I could launch into a new life I had to get down the mountain. I decided the only route to take with my spirits high was the Stirrup Crag descent. This descent (and ascent if you are coming the other way) has a reputation for being rather tricky, but I did not think it could be trickier than the ascent near Bell Rib so off I went. It was a scramble, and legs, hands and bum were needed to ensure a safe ending! Once down the rocky section, however, it was a very pleasant stroll down the Overbeck valley to rejoin the path where it branched off towards Bell Rib to descend the original grassy path. You can avoid all the rocky scrambles on Yewbarrow by using alternative paths and if you do not enjoy that type of climb I would recommend you do that. For those with a bit of adventure in their hearts, do the rocky paths! Exhilarating!

As I arrived back at the car, the sun was still shining, the water in Wastwater was glistening and all was well with the world. My favourite mountain – Yewbarrow.

The Scafells.

Mellbreak from Hencomb.

Loweswater.

Mellbreak

Mellbreak is just pipped to the post by Yewbarrow. It is a fantastic climb with some of the best views around, in my opinion. It also has the advantage of starting from Loweswater village near the Kirkstile Inn, an excellent pub. It is not one of the highest (it stands at 1,676 feet/510 metres) but if you climb it from the Kirkstile side, it is a really feisty fell and, for me anyway, more exhilarating to climb than many of the higher and more famous ones.

I always park near the red telephone box on the edge of the road – as an early starter for walks I can usually get a space there. There is a National Trust carpark a bit further up the road. The route follows the road past the church and pub and then through a small wood to get to a clear track. Much of the time there are also some extremely pretty cows in the surrounding fields (safely on the other side of the wall!).

I have climbed Mellbreak many times now and each time, the steep part of the path through a belt of woods to get into open pasture always catches me by surprise. It is only short, but very steep and you start to imagine how steep the rest of it is going to be. Once in the open pasture, you can see the route directly ahead and yes, 'steep' is the word – you cannot see from there how a route up the scree and rock-scarred face is possible, but I promise you it is. For me, the most difficult part is the grassy slope to get to the foot of the rocky path, but once that part is done (only a few hundred metres) the rest of the climb is an absolute joy. The first time I climbed it, I started the ascent of the rocky path and I could see a couple emerge from the wood belt. They sat down and looked up at where I was and I could tell they were having the same thoughts as me – how on earth can you scale that?

As I climbed, I started to see the views opening up behind me to Loweswater. Each step upwards saw ever-improving views extending further and further with each metre I gained. The rocky path ended and the next part of the route was not as clear as it was up a heathery and scree-like gully. It was a case of hanging onto edges and heather and being very sure of your footing before taking each step, but it was exhilarating. I love that type of climb – unlike the open scree on Grasmoor, being in a gully made it feel a lot safer! The couple who had stopped for a rest just outside the wood were still there and I remember thinking if they did not get started soon they would never get anywhere! Then I realised they were probably waiting to see if I made it safely to the top of the scree before they ventured onto the path! Given how impossible the climb looked from where they were, I cannot say I blamed them.

Once at the top of the gully, there was a ledge with the first full views of Loweswater and the surrounding fells. It was a beautiful sunny day and it took my breath away (of course that could also be because I was out of breath from the climb!) The walk was in stages after that as each new ledge was reached. When I got to the ridge, as well as having Loweswater still well within view, Crummock Water and the Grasmoor mountain range came into view for the first time. It was really stunning. Crummock Water is my second favourite lake (after Wastwater) as I have many happy childhood memories of sitting on the shore paddling with my sister. I remember clearly I had a navy blue swimming costume with a little white ruffle skirt around it – I had superb taste even at an early age. I still also love looking at the Grasmoor scree as even though it was a scary experience, I look at them now with a sense of wonder and pride that I climbed them!

I was close to the top now and the path remained in a gully for most of the route – steep but highly enjoyable and then opened up onto a heathery path for the last few hundred metres to the cairn on the North Top of the fell. The true summit is the South Top at about two and a half metres higher than the North. While it was a bit wet and boggy in places, it was a delightful stroll to the South Top with even more extensive views of the valley towards Fleetwith Pike and Buttermere. The reasons Mellbreak is such a favourite of mine are the panoramic views in all directions, the scrambling climb and the proximity to Crummock Water. What was also amazing were the different colours and textures of the surrounding fells – from grey and red on the harsh screes, to soft greens and yellows on Hencomb with various shades of blue reflecting in Crummock Water from the sky. Fleetwith Pike was a dark shadow ahead and I could see to the coast in the opposite direction.

My route down took me to the Crummock Water shore. The official path seemed to go way off to the right though, whereas I wanted to go to the left. It did not look too steep so I went 'off piste' and straight down the slope to the shore. It was not kind on my legs as I had underestimated how steep it was. The sheep looked a little surprised to see me as well and if the bracken had been in full splendour it would have been impossible! This was the first time I had been that side of the lake and it was superb. There is a slightly more sinister side to Crummock Water that it is hard to imagine when you sitting there enjoying the beauty of it. In 1988 the body of Sheena Owlitt was found, weighted down by an engine block. Sheena's body had been there three weeks before it was found by amateur divers – her husband confessed to her murder. A really odd contrast that such a tranquil place could have such a dark story.

After a short walk, there was a little island outcrop (not quite an island as it had a narrow gravelly link to the shore) and I went out onto it and sat and looked in awe at the fells in front of me – Grasmoor, Whiteside and Rannerdale Knotts to name just a few. I had the place to myself as there is not a road that side of the lake. It was difficult to drag myself away, I have to say.

I did eventually leave, however, and walked back along the lake shore to the Kirkstile Inn. It was a wonderful walk along the shore – several small streams joined the lake so the sound of trickling water and the ducks on the lake was lovely. A magical day ended with a drink at the Kirkstile Inn in the sunshine overlooking Mellbreak.

Hellvelyn via Striding Edge

I had already climbed Hellvelyn as part of the range from Dollywagon Pike to Clough Head. However, I really couldn't get a sense of the climb as it was the third of ten fells (nine Wainwright's) and it had been misty on the top so I had not been able to appreciate the views. It is one of the highest Lake District fells, so is a serious challenge in its own right. The most famous way to climb Hellvelyn is via Striding Edge, so I decided I may as well try that – after all, how hard could it be? The route I planned began in Glenridding and went

Mellbreak from the Kirkstile Inn.

Striding Edge. Photo by Raymond Greenhow.

over Birkhouse Moor then via Striding Edge to Hellvelyn and back down via Swirral Edge and Catsycam (that sentence feels like a different language, so for those reading without a particular knowledge of the Lake District, I was going to climb three mountains and include two very narrow and high ridges on the way).

I got lost for the first hour before I even started (although it meant I explored the lower slopes of the fells around Lanty's Tarn and various interesting wooded areas). When I did start the route, I could see it going to be a popular one as there were many people already on the well-trodden path, but given that ahead there was one of the most difficult ascents I had attempted, I felt reassured by their presence. It was rather a misty day, but it came and went in patches and I remained ever hopeful of good views at the top.

It was straightforward climbing to Birkhouse Moor, although most people stayed on the Hellvelyn path and did not take the detour to the other fell. The most interesting thing about the summit of Birkhouse Moor is it afforded me my first view towards Striding Edge and the challenge ahead. It also showed Swirral Edge but I tried to focus on the first challenge and not get distracted by the second one! There was also an excellent view of Red Tarn, which sits in the dip between Hellvelyn and Catsycam. I am not sure why it is called Red Tarn – I did not see anything red about it. This Red Tarn is not to be confused by the Red Tarn between Pike O'Blisco and Crinkle Crags (see Chapter Two: Divided by a Common Language for more on that).

The route off Birkhouse Moor takes you to a famous part of the Helvellyn route – the 'hole in the wall'. This is not an oddly located cash point, it is in fact exactly what it says – a hole in the wall with a large stile across it. It also pretty much marks the beginning of Striding Edge. It is a view Wainwright saw for the first time on his first full mountain-walking visit to the Lake District. The mist meant the view of Striding Edge kept coming and going, but part of me thought this was a good thing as it meant I could not properly see how scary it was ahead and had to focus on the here and now. The first third is fairly straightforward and you can decide whether to walk right on the top of the arête or take the slightly less exposed path a little below. I spent most of my time on the very top on the basis that if I was going to do it, I may as well do it properly! As I got about halfway, a couple who were walking the opposite way came towards me. The woman looked absolutely terrified and was being led by the hand for every step. She was clearly not enjoying it one bit and her partner said she was scared of heights and had not been keen to do the route. Well, what on earth was she doing here then? It is not a place to be if you are not keen on heights. Striding Edge is dangerous and if you have any doubts, do not attempt it. I gave an encouraging smile to her and carried on as I really did not know what to say.

The views of Red Tarn when they were available were excellent and when I did see Striding Edge ahead, it looked very eerie, but I was making good progress and started to wonder what all the fuss was about. As I got to the last part of the narrow ridge, a man coming the other way told me to keep to the left in the descent of the ridge as someone had been killed on the right a few days ago; there is a memorial to someone who was killed many years before as well! That refocused my mind and put an end to any complacency on my part!

The large step down the end of the ridge was very tricky – how anyone does it with short legs I will never know. It is largely a problem-solving exercise and making sure you have the appropriate leg on each ledge before you reach for the next one. A lift here would be helpful. I got down safely and looked up.

As I stood at the foot of the final ascent of Striding Edge to reach the top of the mountain, with the mist enveloping me and only allowing vision of a few metres, I confess I wondered what I was doing here. Striding Edge is one of the narrowest ridge routes to the top of any Lake District mountain and it has claimed many lives. The memorials dotted around are a strong reminder of the perils of this mountain. Even hardened fell-walkers would remind you to always be careful on this climb.

Ah, I see... this is what all the fuss was about! I did not believe it was possible to scale this rock face. I am no rock-climber and have no wish to be. I heard voices on my left, however, and peered through the mist to see where they were coming from. Hard though this is to believe, there were people further up mending the footpath! They were standing on the rock face handling large pieces of rock, tools and chatting happily about what they were doing.

The Fix the Fells project

The Fix the Fells project is a partnership project with the National Trust, Lake District National Park Authority, Natural England, Friends of the Lake District and Nurture Lakeland. It receives support from local businesses, local communities and visitors, as well as a lot of committed volunteers. Fix the Fells play a vital role in repairing eroded footpaths, protecting the fells from further erosion and protecting the ecology of the Lake District to ensure we and future generations can enjoy walking among the fells. It is a highly skilled job. Please do support them and ensure you treat the fells and footpaths with respect.

To think that while I had been worried about climbing it, these marvellous people had been fixing it gave me great confidence and comfort knowing they were there, so I began my scramble up the steep rock face taking it one step at a time and watching my footing carefully.

It was a real case of keeping three points of contact for the first part of the scramble and pulling myself up, but after a few minutes the path became more evident and slightly less steep, although caution was still necessary. At last the path emerged onto the flatter summit and I started to feel exhilarated for having conquered something I was a bit scared about. There is a memorial on the path just before the summit for a man who was killed on Hellvelyn many years ago and his dog stayed with him, guarding his body until it was found – a very touching story of the bond between dogs and people. There is another stone plaque near the summit cairn that marks where two brave (or perhaps foolhardy!) airmen landed an aeroplane on the summit back in 1926. I know the summit is flat but it is not an obvious place to land an aeroplane!

Swirral Edge.

It was very cold on the top and the large wind shelter was very welcome! The mist was still intermittent, but at various points the views were extensive and looking back over Striding Edge was superb, as well as along the Hellvelyn range towards Blencathra and across the valley to the fells beyond Thirlmere Reservoir. Although Hellvelyn is a flat summit, there is something about it that fills you with a sense of achievement, whatever route you have taken. I gather from reading various guide books and talking to more local people that there is rarely a day when no one visits the summit of Hellvelyn. I can see why – it is a great fell.

I have to say I would not be keen to do Striding Edge the other way; I think going down the scramble would be even worse than climbing up it! My day was not over yet though and I headed off to Swirral Edge and the route to Catsycam. Swirral Edge is nowhere near as narrow or as exposed as Striding Edge, but it still needs to be taken seriously. The path, in places, is not obvious and you have to scramble on parts of it. It is much shorter than Striding Edge though, so if you want to try a narrow ridge but are not ready for Striding Edge, then Swirral Edge is probably a good alternative.

Catsycam was only a short climb and the whole route had views back to Striding Edge and down to Red Tarn. You can also see most of the rest of the Hellvelyn range heading towards Keswick. I took the route down via Red Tarn – it is beautiful – and then the valley route back to Glenridding.

I am glad I conquered Striding Edge. I have a real sense of achievement about it. I would be quite happy to do this route again, preferably in nicer weather. I have not tackled Sharp Edge, which is a similar ridge on Blencathra, but I will do it one day. As for Jack's Rake, well that story is to follow (see Chapter Seven: My Favourite Fells (Part II)).

Steeple (as part of the Mosedale Horseshoe)

I love Steeple, but it would be wrong to write about this fell in isolation as I did it as part of the Mosedale Horseshoe. This journey started from the pub at Wasdale Head and went up the Black Sail Pass route to Pillar and then onto Scoat Fell, Steeple and ending on Red Pike with the Dore Head Screes (more of that later!)

It was a dubious day weather-wise and I was not sure if I would end up in rain and cloud or if it would hold off. As I have said before, however, when you visit the Lakes from Kent/Sussex, it is such a long way that you want to get out of the fells as often as possible even if the conditions are not ideal. Great Gable, at the head of the Wasdale Valley had cloud on the very top of the fell but Kirk Fell and Yewbarrow looked clear. Off I set along the path towards Pillar. I did this route in September 2010, before I had GPS, so I had my Ordnance Survey map to hand and my Wainwright book in my rucksack. The path through the valley along the foot of Kirk Fell was very gentle and there was a sense of intimacy with the fells around. If I knew at this point what I knew about five hours later, I would have paid more attention to the route down the Dore Head Screes that separates Yewbarrow from Red Pike. However, I went on in blissful ignorance around the corner to head up to the ridge leading between Kirk Fell and Pillar. As I had a view stop after a particularly steep bit at around 335 metres, a guy passed me heading up to the dip between Kirk Fell and Pillar. At this point, the path splits between a shortcut that bypasses the dip and arrives further along the shoulder of Pillar and the longer but less steep route to the dip. I decided on the shortcut (I know, once again, I never learn!). The guy passing me headed on up the longer way. He stopped briefly to say hello and said he was a 'slow plodder' who just kept going. I admire people who can keep walking without hardly taking a breather, but it is not a style that suits me as I have said. I admit I did have a rather competitive streak at this moment, however, and decided I would see if I could get to the rejoining of the two routes before he did.

My route was incredibly steep and on a diagonal path. I pushed myself really hard (still with a lot of view stops) and kept an eye on the guy I was racing for as long as he was in sight. When I arrived on the ridge, I could not see him so I was not sure whether he had passed me or not. I was extremely out of breath at this point though, so sat down to recover. As I did, the guy came into sight and as he approached me stopped to chat. I had got there first but there was no doubting that he was breathing less heavily than me! Youth is not everything when you are climbing mountains! That would have been the end of that part of the journey except this random man on the fell changed my walking life forever (see Chapter Eight: Getting Lost! for why).

The man headed off up Pillar and I began again soon after with absolutely no expectation that I would catch him up (and I never did). It was still a surprisingly long way to the summit of Pillar even though I did the direct route and not the Climbers' Traverse. The weather also started to close in and whilst I was not in cloud, I lost the views of the fells surrounding me. On reaching the summit I took shelter in the wind-shelter and looked at the map for the next part of the route. I wanted to stay on the summit longer to wait for the views to emerge but I was anxious about being caught on such a high fell without visibility. This is my point about GPS – since I have been using it, my anxiety levels when the weather closes in are much less and I feel much safer climbing in misty and cloudy conditions. This does not mean I am complacent as that would be more than foolish, but it means I can always find the path even when it is intermittent and always know what route I am heading in.

I headed towards Scoat Fell. There was nothing arduous about the route but the first few hundred yards were extremely rocky and treacherous for that reason. Falling on your knee or ankle could lead to a call to Mountain Rescue, so take care if you do this route. As I got to the Scoat Fell summit, the weather cleared again and I could see for miles once again, with Kirk Fell and, beyond it, Great Gable opening out and the view down the valley I had recently climbed. It was a pleasant summit but nothing that really stood out in my mind. The next part of the walk was to Steeple.

Now, I had no greater expectations of Steeple than any other fell I had climbed. I had not really heard of it prior to deciding to climb the Wainwright's and it does not appear in much literature about the fells. However, it was a delightful short walk and climb to the top and the only word to describe it is 'sweet'. Steeple is a sweet fell and the summit is tiny. There

Steeple.

was a superb view down Ennerdale Water and this was the first fell walk I had done from which I saw that marvellous valley. As I arrived, a couple who had been on the summit said to me 'We will leave you to enjoy this view on your own – we did so it is only fair you do as well'. How lovely! I have never met anything other than nice people on the fells. I sat on the top of Steeple on my own for ages, just drinking in the view. As another couple approached the summit, I in turn moved off to afford them the same intimacy and solitude that I had enjoyed.

I had to return over Scoat Fell again as my next fell was Red Pike. According to Wainwright, this was only 60 metres of ascent from Scoat Fell to Red Pike. It felt like a lot more, perhaps because I had been walking for a while at this point, but it seemed to take a long time and was very steep. I got there eventually though and was rewarded with yet more wonderful views and it was fascinating to see Yewbarrow from the other side. I searched in vain for the armchair-shaped rock that is supposed to be visible on Red Pike and provide a seat for looking at the superb views. I had no luck, but as you will gather from the rest of this walk, my powers of observation are sometimes limited. It was a steep descent to the dip between Yewbarrow and Red Pike at the top of the Dore Head Screes. At this point I was uncertain about whether to tackle Yewbarrow (which I had not climbed) or whether to descend via the scree. I decided, on balance, I was too tired to do anymore 'up' and the Stirrup Crag route up Yewbarrow looked pretty challenging. Besides, once I got down the other side of Yewbarrow there would be a long walk back to the car at Wasdale Head. I am glad from one perspective that I made that decision as it meant I had the most wonderful climb of Yewbarrow at a later date. However, to think that the route I chose was less tiring was utterly misguided.

A stream bubbling like champagne.

Now, according to what I had read about the Dore Head screes, there is supposed to be a grassy path next to it that is easier than the scree route. Well, I searched and I searched for this path and could not find it, so followed another couple down the initial part of the scree. It was pretty scary actually and very steep. For about two-thirds of the scree I went down on my bottom as I did not feel secure enough standing up; it felt like one wrong step would end me catapulting to the foot of the fell in quick, but probably fatal, time. Anyone watching from the valley must have wondered what on earth I was doing. It was only for the final third that I felt brave enough to stand up. The couple I had followed down the steep

bit had been out of sight for most of the descent as it was so steep, but I could not see them in the valley either by the time I stood up – they must have found the grassy path and got down a lot more quickly. I looked again for the path but saw no evidence of it anywhere!

When I eventually got to the foot of the scree (sore, tired and with aching legs), I looked back up at the whole scree. Had I really done that? After all my waxing lyrical about not going near another scree after Grasmoor? So it would seem! I should add that from this vantage point I still could not see the path so decided it was a myth and made my tired way back to the Wasdale Head pub for a well deserved shandy. (Yes, I do cringe everytime I say 'shandy' but it is so refreshing!). As I sat outside on the picnic table, a little robin started to take peanuts out of my hand to eat – it was so sweet! He landed on the table and I would take a peanut out the bag and hold it and he would come and take it and fly it up to his nest. I flattered myself that I have a natural way with cute birds and animals... I rather suspect, however, that this was a very clever little robin who had done this many times!

So, of the whole Mosedale Horseshoe, Steeple is the fell that has made it into my favourites. I plan to climb it from Ennerdale direct next time. A cracking little fell.

I should end this particular chapter with a postscript. In December 2011, I climbed Kirk Fell and came down the Black Sail Pass the other side of the valley from the Dore Head scree. While there was snow around, I looked once again for the path I missed and once again, I just could not see it. It must be there! Where on earth is it?

Chapter Six: Escaping the Fells – Where Else to Visit

If I have not persuaded you by now to try a mountain or two (be they low or high) but you want to see some of the wonders of the Lake District, then I have some recommendations for places that have captured my imagination or heart over the last 30 plus years. Apart from anything else, the towns and villages are good alternatives to walking when the weather is not being kind.

Wastwater and the Wasdale Valley

The striking screes and towering high fells of Great Gable and the Scafells makes this lake a joy to visit. It is the deepest lake in England, surrounded by the highest mountains. There are packhorse bridges, streams and rivers, stunning views and even an island close to the shore to explore. The pub at Wasdale Head is a fantastic place (and has free wifi, which, given it is one of the most remote places in the Lake District, is amazing!). The village of Nether Wasdale has great pubs as well and is very picturesque.

Carrock Beck

Carrock Beck is a little gem in my view. This is a charming ford over a narrow road with a foot bridge and the beck running over the road. You get to it by taking the Mungrisedale road from the A66 and just keep going until you reach a fork in the road and then it is on the left. Take your wellies with you as it is a great place to paddle (or bare foot if you do not mind the cold!). I recommend having a picnic here but it loses the sun by mid/late afternoon, so do not leave it too late in the day.

Keswick

No visit to the Lake District would be complete without a visit to Keswick. I usually stay in this area. With Skiddaw as an imposing backdrop, you could not wish for more. There are great tea-rooms and pubs, as well as a theatre, museum and activities for children along with a street market on Thursdays and Saturdays (go to the Moot Hall for more information). The outdoor shops are great and a short walk from the town centre brings you to Derwent Water where you can hire rowing boats or go on a boat trip. A further short walk along the lake shore in the Borrowdale direction takes you to Friar's Crag, which is a little piece of shore jutting out into the lake giving excellent views across the lake to Borrowdale, Catbells and the surrounding fells.

Haweswater Reservoir

Haweswater Reservoir is a remote lake in the far east of the Lake District that takes a long time to get to but is well worth the effort. Being remote, it is usually quiet and the only

Wastwater.

people around will be walkers destined for High Street, Harter Fell or Kidsty Pike. The opposite shore to the road is part of the Coast to Coast walk from St Bee's to Robin Hood Bay. Haweswater can only be reached by a no-through road that terminates at the head of the lake at the foot of High Street and Harter Fell.

My first memory of climbing a fell in the Lake District is High Street from Haweswater, near the home of the last Golden Eagles and it was in the summer of 1984 when a drought had swept the country. Reservoirs were extremely low and there were hosepipe bans and water restrictions in many areas. This included the Lake District, which, given it includes the wettest

inhabited place in England, is rather surprising! Haweswater Reservoir was created in the 1930s to provide water to the city of Manchester and other urban areas. The village of Mardale was flooded in order to create the reservoir. This caused much controversy, but the Manchester Corporation were successful in their campaign and secured an Act of Parliament that meant the dam was created and the village duly flooded. A final service was held in the local church with over a thousand people present (mainly outside the small church) and the dead, buried over the centuries in the graveyard, were exhumed and taken to the village of Shap for re-burial. Walls were taken down and the local pub, church and houses dismantled, with some of the stone being used in the construction of the dam. The village was deserted and then flooded.

Me on Carrock Beck bridge.

Keswick at Christmas.

Haweswater

High Street was a long grind for someone of my age, although I do recall enjoying the views at the top as it was a beautiful day. But my over-riding memory of that day was the drought. With the exception of the odd puddle, Haweswater Reservoir was empty where the village had been (there was still water nearer the dam). I walked with my mum, dad, brother and sister around the ruined walls, saw what remained of the church and it was fascinating to see this ruined village re-emerge. We even walked over the old bridge that had remained largely intact. I have never done that before or since and it was like being in a desert except rather than sand, there was cracked earth. It was an amazing sight!

Loughrigg Terrace and Grasmere

Loughrigg Terrace near Grasmere will give you wonderful views across Grasmere Lake, Rydal Water and up the valley towards Dunmail Raise with Seat Sandal, Helm Crag and Steel Fell. From Red Bank (limited parking, especially in summer), it is only a short stroll to the terrace.

If you take the opportunity to visit the village of Grasmere then it is a great combination. Like many other places in the Lake District, Grasmere has some lovely cafés, quirky shops and small art galleries. You can also find the former homes of William and Dorothy Wordsworth (Dove Cottage and Allan Bank) and the church where they are buried. There is a pretty stream running through the village centre and it is the start point for many walks, but it is also a place to spend a lazy morning or afternoon browsing.

Tarn Howes

Tarn Howes is a very popular tourist destination and rightly so as it is very pretty. Whilst it is mainly man-made rather than natural, it looks beautiful. If you wish to avoid crowds then an early morning or out of season visit is the best time to go, but even then do not expect solitude. You can walk around the tarn (two miles on excellent paths) or you can sit and admire it from the shores.

Crummock Water, Buttermere and Honister Slate Mine

From Crummock Water, not only do you get a great view of Mellbreak, the views across the lake to the Buttermere range and beyond those to Starling Dodd and Great Bourne, but there are also several places you can sit along the shore and soak up the atmosphere. Stopping off at the village of Buttermere on the way there is worth doing and if you are up for driving over one of the many Lakeland passes, then head over Honister pass and stop off at the Honister Slate Mine. There is plenty of indoor and outdoor entertainment, a great little café and (my particular favourite) a shop that sells a variety of slate objects from wine racks to coasters, along with jewellery, maps, ornaments and gifts.

Hard Knott Roman Fort

The Hard Knott Roman Fort on the Hard Knott pass is a good place to visit if you are interested in history as I am. If you look around the site, you will find various information boards that explain the layout of the site from the ablutions to the Commandant's House. Parts of the ruined walls remain, some of which have been restored. The best view of it is actually from the top of the Eskdale Harter Fell, but exploring it is fascinating. The soldiers inhabiting this fort must have been extremely resilient to cope with the climate they had to endure in the winter at that site, particularly coming from a much warmer country, but you can see why the site would be ideal as you could see any hostile approach for miles around.

Coniston

The boating area of Coniston is another great place to go if you want to venture onto the water. It is next to the Bluebird Café and along a no-through road from Coniston village. You can hire little motor boats or take a ride on the National Trust's Steam Yacht Gondola, which has been restored to its full glory. It was originally launched in 1859 and you can get off at various jetties and explore Brantwood, the home of John Ruskin (a leading art critic and architect in the Victorian era), the Monk Coniston garden or even walk to Tarn Howes. I remember being with my sister in an inflatable dinghy on a rope tied to my dad's deckchair on several occasions (we were not competent enough at that age to master oars or rowing!) Or, if you do not want to venture onto the water, there are lake shores to walk, ducks to feed or a café in which to sit and watch others be active. This is a great part of the lake.

View from Loughrigg Terrace.

Crummock Water.

Coniston.

Forest walks and mountain biking

There are plenty of forest areas for those who wish to stroll through the trees, go mountain biking or even try some of the adventure areas that exist. Trees also cover many of the slopes of various fells, having been planted during and after World War II, and there is a lot of forestry activity in the Lake District. The Forestry Commission is responsible for many of them. Most of the trees planted during this time were evergreen and fast-growing trees not indigenous to the Lake District and there has been a move for many years to reintroduce native trees to these areas. The Wild Ennerdale Project for example, that is supported by the Forestry Commission, the National Trust and Natural England, among others, aims to let the area of Ennerdale develop naturally and reduce human intervention.

Perhaps two of the most well-known forests are Grizedale and Whinlatter. There are lovely walks and more energetic activities at both these forests and the textures are beautiful.

Ennerdale Water

I have to mention Ennerdale Water as my recently rediscovered hidden gem of the Lake District. As it is more remote than some of the other lakes, it is quieter and surrounded by craggy fells and green forests. On a sunny day it is spectacular. I cannot for the life of me work out why I had forgotten this lake and not been there for so long. I will not make that mistake again, that is for sure.

Watendlath

The tiny hamlet of Watendlath is set in a beautiful area up a long, narrow no-through road near Ashness Bridge on the road to Borrowdale. Nervous drivers may find the road a bit of a trial (you need to be able to reverse confidently and well if you meet a vehicle coming the other way), but there is a carpark at Ashness Bridge, buses pass on the main Borrowdale road regularly and you can even get a boat on Derwentwater to the jetty nearby. It is about a two-mile walk from the main road. Once you get there, however, there is the beautiful Watendlath Tarn and within a few minutes stroll, you are up among fells without a road in sight. There are many easy walks in the area. Those looking for more adventure can head to the higher fells of Ullscarf and on to the Langdale Pikes. There is a tea room but, having been there many times, I have yet to work out the opening hours, so do not count on it! When it is open it is lovely and you can sip a cup of tea or hot chocolate looking out towards the fells. Who could ask for more?

These are just a handful of suggestions – there are plenty of leaflets, guide books and online information providing much more detail and many more ideas. Even if climbing mountains or doing long walks is not your thing, or if you have children to take into account, there is plenty to see and do – you can get a sense of the Lake District and the views it has to offer without too much effort.

Ennerdale Water.

It is not all about walking or sightseeing either. When I am not wandering the fells, I take the time to enjoy the local cafés, bars, pubs and restaurants in the Lake District. There is a huge variety and there are lots I have never tried (perhaps this could be my next challenge now I have completed the 214 Wainwright's?) The local produce ranges from cheese to preserves, from lamb and beef to vegetables and is superb. Many pubs and restaurants support local produce so please try and do the same to support the Lake District economy. For beer fans, there are numerous local and microbreweries producing excellent quality beers that have wonderfully creative names! Just look at the labels on the beer pumps in the pubs to see what I mean! I myself am not really a knowledgeable beer drinker (although I

do enjoy them) but several of my friends and family are, so I have it on good authority that the bitters are excellent and certainly I never complain at the odd tipple.

Some of my favourite haunts
Each of the following are wonderful in their own way.

Dog and Gun (Keswick)
I love the food (Hungarian goulash in particular) and the atmosphere, but the bitters are great too. It is always bustling and filled with walkers and lots of dogs. It is the only place

I have been to where sharing tables if you cannot get your own one is the norm and I have met lots of interesting people that way.

The Jumble Room (Grasmere)

This is more for special occasions (an opportunity to wear heels) as it is a restaurant rather than a pub (although the fish and chips are great!). It is very quirky with pictures and jumble all around. The food and atmosphere are great (and I can recommend the prosecco).

Lucy's (Ambleside)

I am a fan of Lucy's restaurant as well as the wine bar across the road. The wine bar does amazing margheritas and the upstairs is cosy and fun. The food in Lucy's restaurant is great as well.

Kirkstile Inn (Loweswater)

Just head for the yellow door. It overlooks Mellbreak so it was always going to be a winner with me. Fantastic for a refreshing shandy or bitter after a fell climb with a great garden in the summer, a cosy fire in the winter and excellent food. Once again, the bitters are recommended.

Drunken Duck Inn (Barngates, Ambleside)

The soup changes every day and is always fantastic. It is my perfect lunch stop. This is where I always push the boat out and have a glass of champagne. The views over the Fairfield Horseshoe from the outside seating area are great and it has its own microbrewery. The way they describe the beers is how you would normally hear wines described.

Horse and Farrier (Threlkeld)

The fish and chips here should be called whale and chips as it is enormous. My first visit here was after climbing the Hellvelyn Range so it was just what I needed to restore my energy. In the summer there is quite a large outdoor seating area on a bank that looks out over some of the many routes to Blencathra and opposite, Clough Head is in its full glory.

Mill Inn (Mungrisdale)

Tucked away but still bustling in the summer. Great food, great beers – a real taste of the Lake District.

Esquires Coffee House (Ambleside)

Just in case you thought all these were bar-related, this is one of my favourite coffee shops in the Lakes. They do the most

Paul relaxing at the Drunken Duck Inn.

amazing Oreo Cookie milkshake (with cream, of course) and there is free wifi access. It now has an upstairs seating area with two large penguins (not real) in the window and giant coffee beans! Well, why not?

The Old Smithy fish and chip shop (Ambleside)
Excellent fish and chips and a real blast from the past for me as my parents used to take us here each holiday. I am delighted it has reopened.

The Bluebird Café (Coniston)
The best hot chocolate ever and stunning views over the Lake. It has recently been refurbished following the floods of winter 2009 and it is now bigger and better.

The Wasdale Head Inn (Wasdale)
I celebrated finishing the Wainwright's here with half a pint of Wastwater Gold. It is a great pub overlooked by the giants of the Scafells, Great Gable and Pillar with a beautiful river running beside it. The beers and food are great and everyone is friendly.

Other places I would recommend: The Pheasant Inn (Thornthwaite); The Queen's Head (Troutbeck); The Langstrath (Stonethwaite); the Tea Shop (Grange); the Doi Intanon Thai (Ambleside); Café 26 (Keswick); The Sun Inn (Bassenthwaite); The Swan and Tweedies (Grasmere); Swinside Inn (Swinside, near Keswick); the Bridge Inn (Wasdale), and the pubs at Nether Wasdale.

I am sure there are many others that I have not yet had the chance to try but I will keep you posted on others as I find them... watch this space via my blog http://heelwalker1.blogspot.com.

The Drunken Duck Inn.

A Brief Interlude: My Favourite Heels

And now for a short break in our Lake District programming for a brief interlude in which I shall be considering my favourite heels. You read that right – I have written about my favourite hills; I also love high heels. Serious fell walkers should probably stop reading at this point as this is my girly side coming out again! I could not keep her quiet any longer.

I own about 40 pairs of shoes in all and most of them are heels. I have loved shoes for years. Bluewater shopping centre is my second favourite place to be after the Lake District and I am doing my civic duty by supporting the shoe shops in these difficult times. I love all types of heels from peep-toes to straps and from boots to courts. I have them in all colours, all materials and they range from bargain basement finds to more expensive (the price of some I have never confessed to my family!). I wear them with pencil skirts, summer skirts, jeans and trousers. Heels are versatile. After much soul-searching, I have captured some of my favourite heels and why. There are dozens of pairs I have seen that are on my 'must-have' list but my finances will not stretch to them (and my house will not fit them in!).

1. My spotty Kurt Geiger shoes with the bow on. These were my most fabulous shoes until the spotty Dune shoes came on the scene. I chose these for my work leaving do in March 2011. It was these shoes that sealed my reputation as the 'Imelda Marcos' of the company I used to work for. I have a long way to go before I can compete with the number of shoes she has though! I have these shoes in pink as well (seriously) and they are so much fun.

2. My black suede Dune boots. These are my favourite winter boots. I actually have two pairs – one I bought this time last year and I liked them so much I bought another pair in the sale that I have not worn yet for when this pair wears out (that is honestly true). Believe it or not, they are very comfortable and I can wear them for work or shopping for hours on end. Until I bought the spotty Dune shoes they were my highest pair (see below). They have just completed their second winter though, so they have been seriously good value and I have saved myself money this year as I do not have to buy another pair (my family call this 'Tanya logic' as to what constitutes saving money, you understand). Walkers talk about walking boots being two or three seasons, but the same applies to heels as well!

3. My spotty Dune shoes with a red sole are perhaps my very favourite. These are my highest, thinnest heels that almost cost a friendship (as my friend really wanted them but they only had my size) and were my very first purchase on ebay. Here I confess I had to practise walking in these before I wore them out as they are seriously high. I am five feet eight inches tall – these make me about six feet two inches! The key to wearing heels though is you have to be able to walk in them otherwise they lose their fabulousness and you just look silly. These are definitely heels for social events and not the office. One of my friends once described them as 'high glamour Minnie Mouse'. A perfect description. Walking in gravel on them is a bit tricky, however, as I discovered outside a local pub in Kent!

Spotty Kurt Geiger.

Black Dune boots.

My highest heels.

Black Buckles – my most sensible pair of heels.

4. My Kurt Geiger black patent leather buckle shoes are, believe it or not, my 'most sensible' pair. These are the ones I wear when I need to tone it down and be all sensible for contract interviews. The heel is slightly wider so is more stable – in ice and snow in particular, they are the 'safest' heels I own. I should say at this point that to date, I have not fallen over in my heels, but in ice and snow I make sure I have someone to cling onto just in case!

5. I also have patent leather shoes of the same style in red, pink and purple. I had to stop there though as they also sell them in black and about three other colours. I thought more than three pairs was becoming excessive (or obsessive perhaps?). I have two pairs in another style that are patent leather with ribbon bows – pink and black. Again, I stopped at two pairs, showing enormous restraint! All these pairs I bought in the sale so they were bargains!

Pink suede and ribbons.

My wellies.

Heels out of town.

6. Last but not least, my pink Kurt Geiger suede shoes with the ribbon. These are possibly my favourite pink pair. I need say no more about them – they are just beautiful.

I try and bring some style to wellies as well. My rather fetching wellies (Welligogs) are pink with black cat footprints on them. There is a splodge of green paint on the toes that happened when I was painting some metal work at a tiger sanctuary (I do some random things). I own two pairs of trainers (one pink pair of course) and I fell over in one pair of them in Tunbridge Wells High Street and twisted my ankle last year. How ironic is that, given I have never twisted an ankle in my heels? Other than the trainers, I do not think I own any shoes that bridge the gap between high heels and walking boots as if I am not in one, I am usually in the other.

I am not sure whether it will be the heels or the hills that finish my knees off, but the combination cannot be good for me. For now though I am still going strong!

Normal service will resume now and I will return to the Lake District!

Chapter Seven: My Favourite Fells (Part II)

So, having eaten, drunk and idled some time away looking around the villages and lakes, you will be refreshed and raring to go to your next fell! Here are a few more of my most memorable fell walks.

Pavey Ark and Jack's rake

I have climbed Pavey Ark twice from the New Dungeon Ghyll Hotel – it is one of the Langdale Pikes. It is memorable to me for two reasons. First is the view of Stickle Tarn, which is second only to the Wastwater view in my opinion. There is a good path to the tarn from the hotel and whilst steep in places, it is not difficult. As I emerged onto a plateau, before me was a simply stunning view. Stickle Tarn glistened dark blue in the sunshine and behind it, the striking rock face of Pavey Ark stood in perfect majesty as though guarding the tarn. To the left, grassy slopes led to the rocky outcrop and crag of Harrison Stickle and to the right, grassy hillocks on the slopes of Blea Rigg and Sergeant Man rose and fell. The sound of the gill (stream) trickling from the tarn back down towards the hotel made the whole scene perfect. I could see people on the face of the crag and assumed they were rock climbers – 'rather them than me' was my thought as a route up did not look possible!

The first time I did this I got to Pavey Ark via Harrison Stickle (another of the Langdale Pikes) and I kept looking back at the tarn as it was so mystical and the sun was catching the water as though it was alive with stars. The view from the top was beautiful and I was determined to come back.

In May 2012 I returned. I had heard a lot about a route up the rock face called Jack's Rake, which makes a diagonal ascent from the tarn to the summit of Pavey Ark. Wainwright dedicates two pages to this ascent and whilst he highlighted that it was tricky in places, it did not seem to be overly difficult so I thought I would try it. It is generally described as one of the few routes where walkers can experience real scrambling. Having done Striding Edge and the Grasmoor screes I felt well prepared. I made my way around the tarn to the foot of Jack's Rake. It was a sunny and dry day, but with each step I started to feel more anxious. All of a sudden, the crag looked much bigger than I remembered and the glimpses of the climb I could see looked pretty scary. I got to the foot of Jack's Rake and looked up at the first section. It looked really steep, but I could see it was possible with care so I took a deep breath and started the scramble.

It was hard – finding handholds and footholds was not easy at that angle of ascent. Wainwright said the average angle was 30 degrees but 50 degrees in the steepest sections. It

Pavey Ark.

Pavey Ark.

Jack's Rake – camera went away quickly after this.

felt more than that to me. I got to the first little ledge, however, and took a photo looking back down. That was the last time the camera came out and the picture does not do it justice. I started the next section, which seemed even steeper with fewer footholds and the rocks above impeding me because of my rucksack. At one point I got half way up one of the sections and could not get any further – there was nowhere to put a foot or a hand so I had to retreat. In such a narrow steep gully without the ability to turn around, I had to find a foothold by trial and error as I could not see. When I got back to the ledge I really could not see the route up this section. I took some deep breaths and tried to climb it with alternative points of contact, namely arms and bottom! With difficulty, I got to the next ledge by a tree (bizarrely located) and looked down the precipice to the tarn.

What was never clear in the literature I read about Jack's Rake was while much of the climb is in a gully and there are rocks to the side, there are plenty of times when you are exposed and falling backwards would mean a sheer drop off the crag. According to Wainwright, as I had reached the third tree the worst was over. He was wrong in my view – it was still terrifying. I started the next section with a large boulder at the top and I was holding on with both hands high up, one foot was stretched out behind into a less than secure foothold and I needed to bring my other leg up to the next foothold. I knew I needed to do that quickly as none of my other points of contact were particularly secure. As I brought my leg forward, my rucksack caught on the rocks above and no matter how hard I tried, I could not get the propulsion I needed to reach the foothold. What followed next was inevitable and there was nothing I could do to stop it. My other foot lost its foothold and I had to use my bare arms to control the speed I slipped down the rocks before I landed at the bottom of the section. This was the first time I have ever yelled in fear on a mountain, but thank goodness that was where I stopped – the sheer drop to the tarn was painfully close.

I looked up at the ascent of Jack's Rake again with my bruised arms and knees already feeling sore. If I am honest, I was actually very scared. What on earth was I doing here? And why on my own? What was I thinking? I am not a rock-climber and have never wanted to be one. This danger was entirely self-inflicted. At that moment I would have gladly traded my walking boots for heels and a glass of champagne somewhere. Going back down was not an option, so I had to keep going. Again I took some deep breaths to steady my nerves and looked up at the rocks in front of me.

There was only one thing for it – I would have to throw my rucksack over the boulder and get up without it. So I did. I had no idea what was above the boulder or where the rucksack would land but at that point it seemed immaterial. Without the rucksack I managed to scramble and drag my way up and over the boulder to another ledge, where my rucksack was fortunately in one piece and safe.

My racing heart started to calm and I felt brave enough to face the next part. The worst really was over at that point. There were further steep drops to the tarn to my left and once at the top of the steep gully section and onto the larger boulders, finding a route was difficult but I did it. As I emerged onto flatter ground (not yet at the summit) I felt the most enormous sense of relief and adrenalin. I got to the summit and sat down overlooking

View from Pavey Ark Summit.

the tarn. I had made it. Never in my life will I go back to Jack's Rake – I did not enjoy it and I have never felt in such danger. Striding Edge and the Grasmoor Screes were nothing compared to Jack's Rake. Since climbing it I have read of the deaths of several people making the same ascent. I really would urge anyone considering it to rethink or if they are determined to do it, make sure you have the right footwear and it is a dry day.

That said, I am so proud of myself for having overcome all my fears and achieved something that plenty of fell walkers far hardier than me have not managed. When I look at Pavey Ark now I cannot believe I did it, but next time I will go another route!

Middle Fell

An uninspiring name for an inspiring fell. I loved this climb and, again, this was not just about the walk but about the mood. Even though it was only March, the early mist seeped away, leaving a beautiful sunny day.

Middle Fell is next to my favourite fell, Yewbarrow in the Wasdale Valley, but they are not connected by a ridge. Unlike Hencomb, which I found a disappointment after climbing its neighbour Mellbreak, Middle Fell is a worthy neighbour of Yewbarrow. As I set forth for the walk, I had a real sense of excitement and anticipation. It looked a great fell.

I parked on the grass at Greendale (not the Greendale of Postman Pat fame) and started the ascent. Whilst steep in places, it was a great climb. Like Yewbarrow, it starts with a grassy slope and turns into a delightful rocky scramble that takes your mind off the fact you are out of breath and focuses it on your next crevice or outcrop to reach for. It also has similar gaps – if you get carried away, they could see you sailing forth on a rather quicker, if more dangerous descent over the Wastwater side of the fell. Please do take care!

As with Yewbarrow, the views open up towards the lake, the Scafells and Great Gable, but with the added wonder of the view of Yewbarrow once you get onto the ridge. Who could complain about a view like that?

The walk along the ridge was a joy, with the sun shining, the lake glistening and here and there patches of snow catching the light like diamonds. These are real moments of inspiration and happiness for me when I feel like I can take on the world. I make some of my most important decisions at these times (although it still takes me ages to decide what I want from restaurant or pub menus).

Given how glorious the day was, I headed onto Seatallen. The route across the dip was rather marshy and it was a bit disconcerting to see the slope to Seatallen looking quite so vertical ahead! It did not look any better as I got to the start of it, but there were helpful footprint ledges in the grassy slope and occasional small mounds that looked good for view stops. I paused a while to admire Greendale Tarn on my left (psyching myself up) and then ploughed on up the cliff, I mean 'slope'. Actually, whilst it was extremely steep, it was not as difficult as I had thought and the footprint ledges made a huge difference. As I arrived at the top I saw the cairn in the distance.

Now, there is nothing particularly special about Seatallen as a mountain – yes the views are good, especially towards the sea and you get a view of some of the more remote mountains such as Haycock from a different perspective and, of course, across to Yewbarrow and Middle Fell. The summit is a rounded dome, which whilst perfectly pleasant, has little of real interest about it. However, the cairn is absolutely enormous! It is 61 metres in circumference and I cannot think of a cairn I have seen that is larger than the cairn on Seatallen. It is the kind of cairn you would expect on Scafell Pike or one of the highest mountains, not on the lesser summit of Seatallen. But there it was – as proud as anything, alongside an Ordnance Survey column. It is thought that the cairn may be thousands of years old and originally built by early British inhabitants.

My route down took me over a third Wainwright, namely Buckbarrow. The ridge walk was divine – a grassy path with wonderful views and it felt like I was on top of the world. It is fabulous when you can walk for miles with little effort and have the whole world in front of you. The ridge takes you via Cat Bields and Glade How before arriving on the summit of Buckbarrow, which has much more to recommend it as a summit of interest than Seatallen, with rocks and crags and lots of little ups and downs.

The route back to the car was interesting! After weighing up the different paths leaving the summit, I chose one that actually turned out to be just a mini stream on grass... I do not

Seathwaite Fell.

Seathwaite Fell and Styhead Tarn.

View from Seathwaite Fell.

Shores of Ennerdale.

even think it had the grandeur of a sheep track! It was too late by the time I realised though as I was half way down the fell. It just petered out above a crag with no hint at a route to avoid the sheer drop in front. I have never been one for rock climbing so I plumped for the left hand side and wound my way down to something that looked like it may have been a path at one point! Below was a river that led from Greendale Tarn and on the fell opposite (Middle Fell, where I had begun) was a very clear path leading all the way in the direction of the car. On that path were a group of walkers and I wanted to have their view of the fell I was on as I was confident there was an obvious path somewhere and I was just not on it!

I found a way down through bracken and then the back fields of a farm to the road and then to the car. As I arrived at the car, I looked back up towards Buckbarrow and there was the path I should have been on! Oh well! I would know next time!

Seathwaite Fell (or 'falling in style'?)

This was a t-shirt weather climb in glorious September sunshine, but it involved a fall that left me with broken dignity!

I started early to make the most of the weather and because the plan was to climb another mountain later that day. So at about 7.30am, I was parked at Seathwaite and walking through the farm towards Stockley Bridge. The route from Stockley Bridge also takes you to more serious mountains, such as the Scafells and Great End. Most people were heading for these more challenging climbs and I doubt anyone woke up that morning with a mission to just climb Seathwaite Fell, other than me. In my view, it is a great fell and I think is only not seen as such as it is a minor fell among its bigger neighbours.

The climb for the first mile was simple enough and very pleasant – there is a good path and the gradients are easy (the first half a mile is a straightforward stroll next to the River Derwent). You could also see the gushing Taylor Gill Force (a waterfall), which was at its best after the recent rains. Now, in his chapter on Seathwaite Fell, Wainwright is quite clear that there are no paths to the top. This remains true from what I could see. He suggests taking the Styhead Pass to gain height and then branch off up the grassy slope. He gives two routes – one being steeper than the other. For once, I decided to take what Wainwright described as the 'easier route' (route B for those who have the books). All I can say is that if mine was supposed to be the easier one, never ever take the alternative route! It looked steep – I was under no illusion it would be anything else, but actually then forcing your limbs up step by step is a challenge. It was made more tricky because the surrounding streams meant the going was wet and slippery. There was clear evidence of people having been that way before me however so if they could do it, so could I!

As I was about halfway up, I took my 22nd view stop and in the distance, down the valley, I could see the whole range of Blencathra and the Skiddaw range just coming into view. It was amazing (I took a photo from the top so you can see what I mean). Such a panoramic view. I also looked down on the constant stream of people on the Styhead Pass heading for greater things than Seathwaite Fell. Occasionally, one of them would look up at me and you could tell they thought I was crazy standing on a near vertical slope without a path. I felt

Sunlight in the forest.

the same at many points on the way up so I understood their thoughts. However, someone else eventually had the same idea as they turned off the pass and headed upwards. It must have been depressing seeing how slow my progress was!

As is always the case, I got to the top and the sight of the cairn as ever, made me forget the pain of ascent. Now, I know I rave about views a lot but the sight of the great slab of Great End, the proximity of Glaramara and Allen Crags and the distinctive Scafell Pike summit in the background, as well as the now full-length view of the Blencathra and Skiddaw ranges, was something many fells higher than Seathwaite cannot boast. It was spectacular (see the photo). I sat on the top for about half an hour just taking it all in. The weather was perfect and warm enough to be basking in the sun. I could have stayed there for hours. The official summit is actually lower than the highest point of the fell which is unusual, but when you are at the top you can see why – sitting at the head of the valley and looking out and the world below warrants the 'official' title more than height.

As I started to leave, a group of about eight guys headed over the fell towards the Styhead Pass. They had been studying maps in the distance for a long time and must have reached a consensus at last! I was slightly ahead of them on the way down. I took it really slowly as on the way up I had thought to myself that the slippery and wet ascent would make a treacherous descent. I took each step one at a time. However the care I was taking, about a third of the way down, I was not careful enough and my feet both slipped from under me and I came crashing down backwards, bottom first, on the grass and rocks. The good thing was, because it was so steep, there was not actually far to fall backwards (forwards would have been a different matter) and my rucksack took a lot of the impact.

My immediate reaction was to leap upwards and look behind to make sure the group of eight guys had not seen (the speed in which I did this was impressive and if there were an Olympic sport at it I would get gold for sure!). Never mind broken bones, bruises or anything like that – pride and dignity first! Thank goodness they must have taken a different route. That would have been mortifying! My next thought was the people on the Pass below... did they see? There were lots of them and any one or more of them could have been looking up at that moment! They were still quite far away though and I decided by the time I got down, if anyone had seen, they would be long gone. My third thought was how muddy and wet I had got in the fall and would it dry before I got to the busy Pass? I decided in the sunshine it probably would and the rucksack would hide some of it.

Finally, I checked for injuries. All bones were intact but my ego was bruised and various parts of my anatomy would undoubtedly join it with bruises over the subsequent days. Sigh! Hey ho though! Onwards!

The rest of the walk was unadventurous but by this time, it was still only about 10am so all those people just starting out thought I was some kind of superwoman as I had clearly finished Scafell Pike already – several of the said 'you must have started early!' I did not enlighten them to what had been my rather less grand mission for the morning! Seathwaite Fell was great and I would recommend it wholeheartedly.

Haycock

I would never have expected this fell to make it into my top 10, but nonetheless here it is in all its glory. It is far from the most popular fell and is one of the most remote to get to, being tucked up in the western fells between Wastwater and Ennerdale Water. I did Haycock with Caw Fell and it was a truly wonderful walk. These two fells were numbers 211 and 212 on my mission of 214 fells and it was day one of two to complete my mission. The sun was shining and it was incredibly warm. I began the route from Bowness Point on the shores of Ennerdale Water, a lake I had completely forgotten the beauty of. The first two miles of the walk took me along the shoreline down to a bridge and it was a lovely walk seeing the deep blue water backed by the rugged crags of Crag Fell and Caw Fell – the water was so still, the mountains reflected in the lake like a mirror. It was hard to tell where the fells stopped and the lake started and I got very carried away with the camera and kept stopping every few metres to take yet another photo (it has become an obsession) – I must have added half an hour to my walk as a result! Totally worth it though!

After crossing the bridge, the path goes into a forest. After another pause to take a photo of some pretty cows and then another pause to take a photo of the sunlight pouring into the forest, creating a purple glow like angels were arriving, I started meandering upwards. Each upward step brought more and more of the Buttermere fells into view behind (worth lots of view stops to regain your breath) and to the left, the fells of Pillar and Steeple. After emerging from the forest, the path turned into a heathery slope and without any particularly steep bits, progress to the ridge was quite fast. From the ridge, Caw Fell is only about two minutes walk away. Arriving on that summit was wonderful and I could see out across the fells to the sea and to the fells of Scotland and the Isle of Man (if my geography

View from the top.

Looking back to Haycock.

is correct) and then inland to fell after fell as they rolled into the distance. The fells on the Isle of Man had a wisp of cloud wrapped around the middle of them like someone had tied a bow around them. It was a lovely view and an incentive to get to the summit of Haycock, which was higher and therefore I hoped would have even better views.

It was less than a mile to the Haycock summit and while a bit rocky in places, there was nothing of any difficulty. And I was right – the views from Haycock were even more spectacular. It was a little hazy, I could see between Pillar and the Buttermere fells as far as Skiddaw and Blencathra in the northern fells, and behind the Buttermere fells even Grasmoor was coming into view. Closer on the southern side I could see the Scafells in all their glory and many of the Wasdale fells, including Yewbarrow. Burnmoor Tarn was peeping out from the slopes of Illgill Head and Scoat Tarn was below, with Ennerdale Water stretching out lazily in the distance. Had I really come up from that far away? Miles and miles of rugged, splendid mountains spread out before me to admire. So I did.

While Haycock is a remote fell and Ennerdale not the easiest place to get to, I would really recommend this fell if you are venturing onto higher fells for the first time. There is nothing tricky about the ascent and the views will impress you if you choose a nice day. The walk along the shores of Ennerdale Water is a lovely introduction and as I went back the same way, a lovely way to end a walk as well. At over 2,500 feet (762 metres) it is a proper fell and you get a bit of everything, from lakes to tarns and from fells to forests. A great mountain.

So these are my favourite fells as it stands in 2012. No doubt some will change as I climb certain ones again in different conditions and via a different route. I firmly believe Mellbreak and Yewbarrow will be in my list for all eternity. They capture the magic for me like no others.

Chapter Eight: Getting Lost!

Now there must be a lot of fell-walkers out there who have been lost on the fells. Even if only briefly; sometimes crags look the same, paths fork at such a small angle that either could be the right one or the mist could come down. All understandable and yes, that has happened to me.

There is, of course, the other type of getting lost, which is when you cannot find the start point in the first place! You may wonder how this is possible but it is surprisingly easy as with one or two exceptions, there are not helpful signs saying 'Armboth Fell this way' etc. You may think that starting lost like this is less common than getting lost on the fells, but personally I am not convinced. I just think people tell stories about it to their friends less often – you can add a bit of exciting ad-libbing to being lost on a mountain with the mist coming down and dangerous crags all around, but that is less true of trying to liven up the story of how you spent hours trying to find the start-point of Hellvelyn from Glenridding village (oh yes... believe me). There is no valour in that I am afraid... I have, however, suffered this inconvenience on several occasions and will share a couple with you (trying to keep my head high rather than hanging in shame).

The first occasion was early on in my fell-walking days when frankly, I was a little over-confident as I had climbed at least five fells when I was a child and I was, after all, equipped with a Wainwright. What could possibly go wrong? The aim was to climb Brock Crags and Angletarn Pikes from Hartsop. All I had to do was park the car, find the filter house (as per Wainwright's guide) and walk up from there. The car was duly parked and I walked into the village of Hartsop. I looked all around for a filter house. Was it that barn-thing? The cow shed? Was that house a converted filter house? How about that path over there... could that be leading from behind where a filter house used to be? This was the first moment when I realised I had no idea what a filter house might look like. After 20 minutes randomly wandering around (whilst trying to look totally confident I might add), I asked one of the residents of the village – pointing proudly to my Wainwright. They looked at me blankly. Filter house? After a few minutes' consideration they pointed me in the direction of a carpark... the penny dropped. I had parked in a different carpark to the one highlighted in Wainwright's guide and therefore was about a quarter of a mile out! I followed the path that appeared to be the right one and after about 15 minutes found the filter house (right next to the river... obviously). This was my first reality check and lesson that I am sure I read in one of Wainwright's books that fell-walking and wishful thinking have nothing in common.

Angle Tarn after I had found my route!

This is what Crinkle Crags actually looks like!

Everything is further than you think! I was expecting the filter house to be visible from the car. Another valuable lesson is never just have a guide book – always take an Ordnance Survey map and a compass. A guide book, however good, is not good enough on its own.

The second occasion really was inexcusable and actually more than a little embarrassing. It was also much more significant and for this one I hang my head in shame! The aim was to climb Crinkle Crags and Bowfell from the Wrynose Pass at the Three Shire Stone. It was a little misty but not too bad. A little knowledge is a dangerous thing, however. I was convinced I knew where the Three Shire Stone was so off we headed (my husband and I) and parked the car. The Three Shire Stone is a famous tall stone built to mark the point where three previous counties met – the counties of Westmorland, Cumberland and

Lancashire. Back in the 1970s, however, the county boundaries changed, which meant the Lancashire boundary moved south and Westmorland and Cumberland were merged into Cumbria. No idea what the purpose was. Seems pretty random to me.

We walked to the point where I thought the stone should have been and I said 'Oh, the stone has gone – how strange!'. Oh well, I knew it was the right place so we headed off regardless in the direction of (as I thought) Crinkle Crags. Before long, the path deteriorated and the grass became increasingly marshy. We ploughed on regardless – our first milestone was to be Red Tarn. It is amazing how I could convince myself that each puddle was a tarn. 'This must be it' I said, confidently looking at a 'tarn' about the size of the pothole outside my house. 'And look – there is a path heading up steeply so we must be right!'

Or not as it turned out. We did indeed head upwards and actually, when near the top, there was another walker heading in the same direction, which further added to my misplaced confidence. Eventually we reached the top after a scramble up some rocks. Hurrah! However, at the top, the picture in Wainwright's book did not look like the top of the fell we were on. It was still misty so we could not see far, but the cairn was different for certain. I peered over my shoulder sheepishly at Paul 'Um… I don't think this is Crinkle Crags', I said. He looked at me with a very puzzled expression as though I was clearly deranged. 'Well, what on earth is it then?' A not unreasonable question – if only I knew the answer. I extracted the Ordnance Survey from the rucksack (yes, by that point in my walking career I had got one with me!) Ah… Pike O'Blisco! Ever so slightly to the right of Crinkle Crags! Paul looked at me with daggers… oops! 'Not to worry' I said cheerfully. 'Look! The mist is clearing and there is Crinkle Crags and, oh yes, there's Red Tarn'. Funny how large it looked and how red the earth around it was; not a small puddle after all it turns out…

It so happened that two days later, we climbed the Coniston Range from Great Carrs and Grey Friar right through to the Old Man and back again. We climbed from the top of the Wrynose Pass again. As we ascended Great Carrs, we looked across the valley and there –as plain as could be – was the Three Shire Stone and a well-worn path leading towards Crinkle Crags. An obvious starting point and path almost shouting out to us it was so plain. How had I got it so wrong? As I said at the beginning – a little knowledge is a dangerous thing. My dad could not believe I missed the Three Shire Stone. When you see it, you will see why!

The moral of the story for me was to get a GPS. Some people dismiss satellite systems as having no place in the kit of true walkers and some people only refer to them briefly as though it is a shameful secret. Well, I disagree. After all, there are plenty of people who said the telephone would never catch on. I read somewhere that if Henry Ford had asked people what transport they wanted, we would have got the answer 'faster horses'. I have only been using GPS since December 2010. The reason I did not start sooner is because I had thought the reception would be poor. I was wrong. I bumped into a guy when climbing Pillar in 2010 who climbs all the Wainwright's over 2,500 feet (762 metres) each year. He said the year before it was so misty he had to rely on his GPS system. I asked him about the quality of reception and he had nothing but praise. He did, however, say he would never use it when the weather was good. Why?

I have not looked back since getting GPS. My current one is a Garmin GPS Map 62s, but there are a range of systems out there varying in price and functionality. I chose one that has buttons on it and is not touch-screen so I can use the buttons with gloves on. I am a good map-reader and I pore over maps and guides of the Lakeland mountains frequently – anything from Wainwright to Cicerone, and from Ordnance Surveys to walking guides and free leaflet maps. I plan all my routes that way and get enormous pleasure from it – that is how I calculate distance, height gained, how long it will take, ridge routes etc. Then I plot it on my GPS. When I walk, I have the relevant map and guide with me, but I rarely refer to them as the GPS tells me exactly where I am (according to my route plan) and the name of nearly every crag and rock around me. Ever had two paths close together and not sure which one to take? Or know you need to head left at a certain point but not sure if the point

My trusty GPS and Ordnance Survey maps.

you are at is the right point? Problem solved! If you go wrong it is clear in seconds that you have wandered off the correct route. If you have got to the right point to turn, it is obvious.

I will also extol the virtues of it in mist. I mentioned my independent streak earlier. My family will tell you it is combined with an enormous degree of stubbornness. They are probably right. It is a long way from Kent to Lakeland and when I am there for only a week, I want to climb as much as possible – whatever the weather. I am sure, if they are truthful, even the most seasoned walker can become disorientated in thick mist. Well, it has happened to me anyway, but GPS kept me on the right route. I would encourage anyone to do the same. It enables me to climb on more days than I would feel confident enough to without it for reasons of weather. It means I do not get lost and – perhaps most importantly – you always know for certain when you have reached the true summit! It is also a very useful tool to provide an accurate grid reference if you need the services of Mountain Rescue. There are a range of GPS systems out there – have a look and who knows? You might even like it!

Chapter Nine: Walking with Children and Animals

Childhood memories

I have extremely fond memories of the Lake District from when I was little. I will say again that I did not enjoy climbing mountains then. As a child who frequently got car-sick (tablets did not help), I had problems being in the car for anything other than short journeys (although I expect this was more of a burden for my parents than me given they had to cope with me!) This is why mum and dad started travelling up early in the morning to the Lakes so that I would sleep for a lot of the journey and, without traffic, it would not take as long (this was before the M25 was built, which was a shock to me as I thought it had been around since the dawn of time).

So I am not looking back with rose-coloured glasses. There were drawbacks. But my over-riding memories are positive. I remember sitting in the river at Wastwater under the packhorse bridge thinking I was so brave to do it as it was so cold (still wearing that same blue swimming costume

Wastwater Packhorse Bridge. (Photo taken by my mum.)

with the white ruffle around the middle). I also remember exploring the island at Wastwater and being scared by how quickly it got deep the other side as you could see the rocks disappear into the darkness. My brother Simon once rowed the dinghy right to the other side of the lake and waved to us from the opposite shore. I was so impressed!

Nowadays, there are many more exciting things for children and families to do: adventure parks; bike riding; horse-riding; ghyll scrambling; numerous water sports; the Honister Slate Mine; castles with birds of prey; and a range of other activities. But even before these came along we found plenty of ways to entertain ourselves. We used to go swimming in Troutbeck at the public swimming pool. This was very exciting and I remember being there in my orange arm bands and rubber ring when I was tiny, then progressing to just the arm bands as I got older (one day I am sure I will be able to manage without those too... ha!) For some unknown reason, my brother, sister and I thought it highly amusing to change the order of the words from 'Troutbeck Bridge Swimming Pool' to 'Bridge Beck Trout Pooling Swim'. I can only imagine we thought we were saying it backwards and how very clever we were! Happy days!

As I grew older, we stayed in self-catering properties in different parts of the Lake District. For the first few years of my memory, however, we stayed in a chalet (number four of four in total) in Skelwith Fold near Ambleside. The site is now a caravan park. I remember we always had that chalet as it was next to the woods where there was an enormous Yew tree that we always tried to climb (I was too little to make much progress!). There was also a little shop in the reception cubicle (it was tiny so you had to ask for things, there was no room to go into it) and each year we arrived, I was allowed a strawberry milkshake. I preferred chocolate milkshakes, but I liked the colour pink so always went for strawberry. Mind you, I liked pink so much I wanted to live in a pink house so perhaps not unexpected (I no longer have that desire).

At least twice in our two-week holiday we would have fish and chips with mushy peas at the Old Smithy in Ambleside and would sit inside to eat them at the picnic tables. I am delighted to say that the chip shop has reopened and is fantastic. I remember feeding the ducks at Bowness and being chased by a swan, sitting by and paddling in numerous lakes and rivers, playing putting in Ambleside and going to the pencil museum in Keswick. They were very happy days and I thank my parents for taking us there so often.

My brother Simon was more of an outdoors person than my sister and I were. How so many children have climbed all 214 Wainwright's is a mystery to me as you would simply never have got me up that many at that age. The High Street route just went on and on and on. Emma and I moaned almost the whole way up with mum and dad saying 'it is just round the corner – just one more "up" bit and then it is the top', which was just not true! It felt like there were about a thousand 'up' bits and the top just would not appear, but then I did have a rather weighty bottom lip in the form of a pout weighing me down that could have made me take longer!

Eventually we got to the top, however it put Emma off mountain climbing for good. She has never climbed another mountain since and has no intention of ever climbing one. She still loves the Lake District though. It is funny that while I did not enjoy that particular climb at that age, it has not had the same impact on me. It is strange how sisters can be so different. The end of this story actually came about three years ago. When I started my mission to climb all the Wainwright's, I asked mum and dad which ones I had already done. Mum listed them – Old Man of Coniston, Skiddaw, Causey Pike, Catbells and High Street. Then the words 'Oh, and of course when we did High Street we did Mardale Ill Bell as well so that is another one you have done'. Mardale Ill Bell as well? Funny how it never came up on the walk itself that we were climbing two mountains! No wonder there were so many ups! Mind you, given how much we complained I cannot say I blame them for not mentioning there was another one after High Street!

I have been on holiday with my nephews since then, but otherwise have had little experience of holidaying with children now I am an adult. That was until August 2011.

Never work with children and animals!

Television presenters often say 'never work with children and animals'. I wonder if the same applies to walking? I did not get my insight into walking with children until recently. In August 2011, I stayed with some friends and their family in Grasmere in a large holiday let. It was an ideal house and the location was superb. In the party were two children aged 10 (Rebecca and Adam), and a large dog (a lurcher) called Clancy. There were usually at least six or seven adults but sometimes more, as it was an open house for friends to join the party.

Everyone seemed to know I was a lover of fell walking. This could be because I arrived at the house at 9am one morning having driven up from Sussex over night and had already climbed a fell. (The fell in question was Dodd by Skiddaw, which I admit is not the largest fell in the world, but even so they were impressed and I was content to let them be so!) So they asked me to plan a route for them to ease them into climbing fells. Fantastic! Always happy to have opinions and this was something I actually knew about! For their first venture into the fells, I chose Castle Crag. A pipsqueak of a fell but with a real mountain feel about it and fantastic views. Off we set along the flat path past the campsite and river and along the Cumbria Way. Just before we went up from the path to start the proper ascent, one of the children, Rebecca, said the age-old words 'Are we nearly there yet?' So soon? We had climbed about four metres! It was followed by the plaintive voice of Adam 'We're not going up theerrrre, are we?' Um... yes...

However, the good news was that Castle Crag has some great story-telling potential as according to Wainwright's guide, there was a hermit called Milican Dalton who used to live in a cave on the fell between the two World Wars. Well, this was like manna from heaven for two 10-year-olds. One of the men in the party embellished the story with a real imagination that I did not know he possessed about how Milican made tools and found things to eat by utilising the nearby stones, rocks, berries and plants. Seriously, even I started to believe it – he was so convincing!

The other good news was that going up the slate path very near the top felt dangerous to them, so they concentrated extra carefully and found it particularly exciting. This

Castle Crag. (Photo taken by my mum.)

Clancy.

Catbells.

kept them entertained almost to the top. Just before the top there is a very strange arrangement of vertical stones that someone has gone to a lot of effort to complete. No one really knows who or why and whenever they are knocked down, they are mysteriously put back. Once at the top, Rebecca and Adam loved it! Looking back, I bet I complained a lot more to my parents than Rebecca and Adam did to theirs and I doubt I appreciated a view at that point, just the sandwiches and bar of chocolate at the top! The dog, Clancy, looked particularly enthused (although that was possibly the food too!).

What was particularly good was seeing how much the adults loved the climb and the views – most of them were not fell walkers and had only climbed one or two fells in the past. It is fascinating watching others slowly getting the bug! They were lucky it was such a lovely day as the views along Borrowdale were spectacular. The cairn on the top is a rock formation that holds a memorial from World War II to the men of Borrowdale.

Anyway! Down we went the opposite side of the fell through woods, beside streams and I was told – at length – the plot behind the final Harry Potter film in a joint effort between

Rebecca and Adam, both disputing the finer points of how Snape died in the film and whether it was as good as how it was depicted in the book.

I thought I had done my bit for family walking, but apparently not. The adults, it seemed, were so full of enthusiasm they wanted me to find another route for them all, but this time, a 'proper' route with real scrambling and more than one fell. Now, people really should not say that to me as I am fell junkie and could climb for miles and miles (with frequent view stops). If people say they want a challenge I take them at their word. Children as well! So I planned a route that, in my mind, would be good for adults but would also be manageable for kids. The route was from Hartsop – up the valley towards Hayeswater, then directly up Gray Crag, on to Thornthwaite Crag then down to Threshwaite Mouth and down the valley back to Hartsop. Simple!

Well! It took three hours to leave the house in the morning what with hangovers, children getting ready, breakfast in about five sittings, making coffee, sandwiches etc etc. So we did not even leave the house until midday. Now for me, this is torture – I like to get out on the fells early and be back down early afternoon for a nice lunch and a glass of wine! If it is a particularly long walk, getting back late afternoon is fine but I always start early. Then when we arrived at Hartsop, it took a further 20 minutes to put on boots, put things in rucksacks, decide who was going to walk with whom and who was in charge of the dog – now, honestly! If they had not been doing all these things in the three hours it took to leave the house, what had they been doing? Final decision – who was going to hold the GPS? Here I put my foot down with my size 6 North Face boot: 'Me'. It was the control freak in me. I am the same with maps.

Finally, off we went. Clancy the dog seemed as merry as anything scampering around, running in the stream and leaping at different blades of grass etc. I was in the lead (you are starting to understand something about my character I am sure… I love taking in the views but we really had to start making progress!). We were heading towards Hayeswater with gusto. At last!

Ten minutes in, Rebecca decided she was too hot and did not want to wear what she had chosen to wear… so, rucksacks were unpacked, lighter clothes chosen and put on and we restarted. Adam decided to jump in the stream as he was so hot. When he came out he was cold and wanted a fleece. Rucksacks unpacked again, fleece found and put on and we restarted. Five minutes later, fleece off and back in rucksack. Then one of the adults wanted a cap… rucksacks unpacked, find the cap. Now we needed a drink and a view stop… oh, look! Yes, that really is the car… isn't it strange how close it still looks…! Deep breaths, change GPS batteries and off we went.

At that point, Clancy decided to roll in something seriously unpleasant, and then he became my new best friend! He decided it was me he really wanted to walk next to all the way and particularly share the kissing gate experience with me. Oh joy!

After two long hours we got to the top of Gray Crag. To this day I have no idea how we managed it, although Adam had enough energy left to do the family dance on the cairn,

Who's Looking at Ewe?

The bravest photo I have taken.

Dogs on Derwent Water.

Lonscale Fell.

which we all joined in with. Rebecca took another few minutes to arrive but she bravely got there with encouragement from another walking party on their way down and joined in the dance. Once again, seeing everyone taking in the views was wonderful to watch. They all wanted to know what the fells were called and I could actually tell them. I never used to know them but always wanted to. It was only when I started climbing fells that the look and order of them slotted into place and now I can name most mountains visible when climbing. I am proud of that. It was nice to be able to share it with people who were loving it as much as me.

Next stop was Thornthwaite Crag. We were all a little tired at this point as it had been a mammoth task to get to Gray Crag. However, it was only a short way and a short climb and once the cairn was in view, energy levels rose again to get to it.

We started the descent. Now, at this point I admit I had not really thought it through. I had done the Cauldale Moor/Thornthwaite Crag dip where Threshwaite Mouth is and as the adults wanted a scramble it seemed perfect. For kids? Not so sure. I give them both credit at this point though that they both managed it. Adam was more of a mountain goat than Rebecca and there was some complaining! But I would have done exactly the same in their position when I was their age. In fact, I know I was worse! Clancy, on the other hand, was up and down it about five times. The only time he looked daunted was when one of the adults called him back and he thought he was going to have to go back up the slope for the sixth time! You could read his thoughts: 'No way am I coming back up there. I've done my climbing. You come to me!' Bless him. Finally, about six hours after we started we got back to the car. Then we went back to Grasmere for a very well earned glass of vino!

As I mentioned at the beginning of the chapter, television presenters often say 'Never work with children and animals'. Given that I usually walk as part of a couple or on my own, I was fully expecting my feelings to be 'never *walk* with children and animals'! However, I am not so sure. There were elements of frustration but these were minor and, overall, I actually think I preferred it. It is nice seeing the happy reactions of others and their sense of achievement. It is also nice laughing at each other and our situation on occasions and being able to talk about the walk and the views. It was nice sharing something I am so passionate about with others. It was also a delight seeing how Clancy was so excited and free. Would I want to walk like that every time? Probably not. Would I do it again? Definitely yes, and my poor (or fortunate) nephews will one day discover this.

I should also add about this particular holiday that the day after the mountain walk, the family decided to go 'ghyll scrambling'. This is pretty much exactly as it sounds – you walk up a mountain (or part of one) and then you come down in the ghyll, which is effectively a river. You scramble down rocks, duck trees, jump into pools and generally get very wet and often totally submerged. You are provided with waterproof kit but nonetheless, no one looked particularly dry after the event! I mention this because the children were exceptionally brave, particularly Rebecca, who was much braver than any of the adults. I firmly believe some of the adults only did some of the more tricky aspects because Rebecca did not hesitate and did everything and they did not want to lose face. On one or two occasions she even went back to do a particular jump or dive again!

I, on the other hand, sat this adventure out claiming poor eyesight and that I could not get my contact lenses too wet (genuinely true but a helpful excuse as I had absolutely no desire to do it – being cold and wet does not appeal!). I admire the bravery of all those who did it though.

Sharing fells with animals

Of course, you do not get a lot of choice about walking with some animals – from sheep to cows and from eagles to jackdaws (and, of course, crows circling the top of Fairfield looking for unsuspecting walkers throwing their frozen sandwiches away!) I love most animals and grew up with various pets around.

The Lake District has some amazing animals – red squirrels have been making a comeback recently after being reintroduced there; one summer holiday I saw four at various points. I never realised how small they are compared to grey squirrels. I have already outlined my love of the deer there. There are also beautiful birds – there is usually a peacock hanging around near the Queen's Head at Troutbeck!

Other than seeing the beautiful deer on Troutbeck Tongue, two occasions stand out in my mind regarding animals in the Lakes. One was on a walk up Lonscale fell from the Skiddaw carpark. It was a really hot and sunny day and Lonscale was the last of the mountains around Skiddaw that I wanted to climb as part of the Northern Fells. There was nothing difficult about the ascent, but the grassy slope from the main path to the ridge was very steep. As I got about two-thirds of the way up, I could see a sheep on one side of the fence and a lamb on the other side. From where I was standing, the lamb looked as though it kept throwing itself into the fence. I could not work out why, other than it was trying to rejoin its mother. Another walker was coming down the path I was on and he stopped and looked briefly at the lamb and then carried on. We said good morning as we passed and I assumed everything was fine with the lamb. However, when I got to him, he was stuck in one of the square fence holes. Each time he tried to back out of the hole his horns were getting stuck. The lamb was clearly very distressed and as I came closer, tried again to throw himself through the fence.

I have to say I was extremely annoyed that the guy I had just passed on the path had not helped this poor stranded animal. The lamb was not small and I was not sure how on earth I was going to help him. I could not leave him like that though, so I took his head in my hands and tried to ease his horns back under the wire and through the fence hole. It was not easy as he would not keep still. However, I did eventually manage to free him – falling backwards with a lamb on top of me. My next task was to make sure he did not just escape and run off as he was the wrong side of the fence – the rest of the sheep were the same side as his mother and he had clearly been trying to get back across to her and them. If I left him the wrong side he would probably do the same again and get stuck again. To this day I will not know how I managed this but I wrestled him over the fence. It was a sight to behold as legs and feet went everywhere (and that was just mine!) and put him the other side without injury to either party. Mother and lamb were reunited and went happily off to join the others – without even a thank you! I, on the other hand, had the rest of the mountain to climb.

The second occasion was climbing Holme Fell, which is a low fell near Coniston. I climbed it from the National Trust carpark at Yew Tree Tarn (free parking if you are a National Trust member as I am). I was not expecting great things from Holme Fell – it is only just tips over the 1,000 feet/305 metres mark and it was still misty even at that low height. But walking in the fells can always take you by surprise.

The walk was straightforward – good paths throughout and easy gradients. However, early on in the walk I went through a gate to get into a field at the foot of the fell and in front of me were about six of the most enormous cows I have ever seen! Their hair had gone fluffy and curly in the rain and while enormous, they looked quite sweet. At the time I thought they were fluffy Fresian cows as they were black and white, but I have since learned they are Belted Galloways. Having said they were sweet, I was very conscious that they were right in my path. I may be a country girl (with a bit of city thrown in) but I did actually stop and draw breath before marching into the field. It was definitely the path though, so off I went. All of about 10 metres further on when lo and behold, there was a bull! No mistaking it – a bull and proud of it with an enormous ring through its nose! It was not looking at me in a friendly way so that was it, I hot-footed it back to the safety of the other side of the gate. I know I try and retain elegance when walking but I lost all decorum and simply bolted. Here, then, was a pickle! I remember a sign on a gate in a field in the village where I grew up when I was little. It said 'Only go through the gate if you can cross the field in nine seconds... the bull can do it in 10'. Now, the sensible part of me knew that was a joke but it stuck with me and I never went in that field. I also remember the very rare story about someone being killed by a cow. It is undoubtedly an unlikely way to die but I was a bit reluctant to take a chance, so I spent a few minutes weighing up my escape routes and the best plan of action if the bull decided to charge at me. It did not look fast (but then I am hardly Linford Christie). The best plan was to dodge it and hide behind a tree in my view. So, after taking a few deep breaths, I took my life in my hands and walked with confidence through the gate (confidence not entirely real I confess).

All the cows and the bull totally ignored me! What an anti-climax! But I cannot say I was disappointed. The rest of the walk was uneventful. I could see Yew Tree Tarn through the mist and some of the close low fells but other than that, the views were not good in such conditions. On the way down I was feeling exceptionally brave (bolstered by my previous cow and bull experience) and stopped long enough (about two seconds) to take a picture of the bull. I was not making up how enormous he was!

There are also lots of dogs who you can tell love being on the fells. I remember my dad having to carry our dog over the rocky part of Causey Pike once as his legs were so little (the dog's legs that is, not my dad's!) Our dog only climbed one or two fells – a Cairn Terrier, he was really too small to tackle many and it would have been too much for him.

One of the most amusing memories I have of dogs on fells, however, was two Labradors in Derwent Water. I was coming back from my first climb of Walla Crag and as I walked around the water's edge, I saw two Labradors playing with a stick in the water. Their owner would throw the stick in and they would both swim out and see who could get there first to get the stick and return it to their owner. They did this two or three times and one of them was a faster swimmer and always got there first. So the next time, the other dog leapt in with the fast dog as though it was just as keen to get to the stick but then it held back, only going about half the distance to the stick and let the fast dog get the stick and start making his way back to the shore. As the fast dog drew level with him, he simply stole the stick from his mouth and bounded back to the shore to return it to the owner. This then happened about three more times and each time, the fast dog did not suspect anything. He may have been faster, but he was not very bright!

I look forward to the day when I have a dog and can take him on the fells – they are wonderful company (but it is important you keep them under control and do not let them hassle the livestock).

Sharing the fells with people

I have also met some amazing people on the fells, whether walking on my own or with others. In the main, walkers I have come across on the fells have been very friendly and some of them very chatty. A few people stand out in my mind – if any of these were you, it was lovely to meet you.

On top of Thornthwaite Crag by the enormous cairn, a guy from Liverpool who had driven up that morning to climb a 'few fells', namely Gray Crag, Thornthwaite Crag, High Street and The Knott. He had climbed up from Patterdale. He was telling us about a photo he had come across in his parents' house that was taken on High Street or 'Racecourse' Hill. In the late 1800s, locals used to gather on top of High Street in their Sunday best to race horses and have picnics. How amazing is that? I knew High Street had a Roman Road but I had no idea about the rest of its history. Sure enough, however, when you look at the Ordnance Survey map, the term 'Racecourse Hill' is used.

On my Fairfield Horseshoe walk when I was struggling against the wind between Great Rigg and Fairfield itself, a man in a red waterproof gave me words of encouragement as he overtook me as he could see I was finding it difficult. I really appreciated those words at that moment (although an offer to carry my rucksack for me would have been even more welcome!).

I have also met some lovely people in the many pubs and cafés in the Lake District. The Dog and Gun in Keswick is always so busy that it is often necessary to share tables. It is then usually inevitable that you start having conversations – it is fascinating what you learn about the Lakes and other parts of the world.

In my experience, nearly everyone says hello or gives a wave if they are further away. I love that. Sharing the fells with other people and animals is lovely.

Chapter Ten: Low Walks and Low Fells

The Lake District is clearly not all about mountains – the Lakes themselves make for some amazing low-level walks. Before I fell in love with climbing fells, I did a lot of lower-level walks and even now still enjoy those.

One of my particular favourites is walking around Thirlmere. This is about 10 and a half miles and there is only a small amount of ascent involved (about 500 feet/152 metres in total and this is in several sections, not all in one go). I used one of the 'Footprint' maps when I did this walk the first time and this was adequate (although do always have an Ordnance Survey map with you as well). The walk starts opposite the Swirls carpark on the main A591 road. There is an initial uphill section as you go through the Great Howe wood and another one at Wythburn on the slopes of Hellvelyn, but other than that, it is pretty much flat. Thirlmere is a reservoir rather than a lake and is used to supply water to Manchester and the North West. It was created in the 19th century and the dam was completed in 1894. The dam itself is amazing – you get the best view of it from the top of Raven's Crag (one of the Wainwright fells).

Thirlmere Reservoir.

Moody Thirlemere from Raven Crag.

Loughrigg Tarn.

I remember the second time I did the Thirlmere walk, a small red car was negotiating the winding road over the dam – it has high stone walls both sides, rocks at the A591 side and some sharp corners. There was much revving of the engine and reversing and manoeuvring and then a rather worrying crunching sound as the metal work scraped into one of the walls. I was trying really hard not to stare, but there were no other cars coming. The road is more than wide enough for a single car so it was a bizarre incident to take place. It really highlights a key issue in the Lake District though – if you drive on the narrow roads,

lanes and passes, you really have to know the width of your car and be able to reverse and manoeuvre with confidence. I have been caught on several occasions on passes where drivers are out of their depth and cause chaos because they cannot do that. Know your limits!

After ten and a half miles, the sight of the end point is very welcome! There are various places to recover, including the Kings Head back on the Keswick road and a range of pubs heading towards Grasemere.

Another superb low-level walk, but this time at a higher altitude with perfect views is **Loughrigg Terrace and Loughrigg Tarn**. If you are lucky enough to be able to park on Red Bank, it is a mere five-minute stroll to Loughrigg Terrace and the views out across Grasmere lake and towards Helm Crag, Steel Fell and Seat Sandal are stunning. You need to see it at all times of day to really appreciate it, although in the evening sun it is beautiful. Loughrigg Tarn is only a few minutes walk from the Terrace back along the road. You can do a circular walk from Ambleside that also passes Rydal Caves.

An excellent low-level walk with a very young child (pre-walking age) is around **Buttermere**. This can be done from Gatesgarth or from Buttermere village near the Fish Hotel. It is four miles and pretty much flat. You have lovely views of Haystacks and Fleetwith Pike ahead of you and the lower slopes of High Stile, High Crag and Red Pike to name just a few. You stay close to the lake almost the whole time and there is only a little road walking involved. At one point you go through a rock tunnel, which I still find exciting as an adult so young children are in their element. I took my nephew around there with my family when he was only about 18 months old.

If you fancy something a bit feistier, then I can highly recommend the walk around **Wastwater**. This is absolutely not for the faint-hearted because it takes you along the foot of the screes and the lake is scarily close should you take a tumble. But if you are up for a challenge without climbing a mountain, then I would say it is one of the best routes you can find. I did this walk about three or four years ago going anti-clockwise from the foot of the lake with my husband. It was a lovely warm day with some sunshine and a cool breeze – perfect walking conditions. Starting from near the National Trust property, we walked along the lake shore and admired the beautiful old and large houses that must have such lovely views. I believe you can rent parts of them for self-catering and there is a youth hostel there as well. It must be quite lonely in the winter but I am sure the location makes up for it.

Very soon, we were on a gravelly path walking along the foot of the lake. This was my first time on this part of Wastwater and looking up the lake to that famous view of Great Gable, Yewbarrow and Lingmell, with the forbidding screes on the right plunging into the lake was stunning. It is my favourite view – my favourite lake and favourite area – all in one picture-perfect view (at that point I did not know Yewbarrow was to become my favourite fell as I had not climbed it). I got very snap happy here but ended up taking a photo that personally, I think could rival some of the most well-known photographers who have captured this view. This is probably the only photo I have ever taken that could do that but I am extremely proud of it. It has not been altered at all – the wispy clouds, the red on the scree, the still water and the clouds mirrored in the lake are all as they were.

Paul eventually dragged me away to continue the walk. It follows the shore for about a quarter of a mile and passes a filter house and boat house and then follows the river away from the lake to cross the bridge further down in the woods and back up the opposite shore. Here, you are at the foot of Whin Rigg, one of the two fells that form the summit of the Wastwater screes. Rather than branching up the Whin Rigg path we carried on along the

Wastwater.

Eerie Easedale Tarn on my first solitary walk.

back of the lake. The views are just always incredible and I will never tire of them – I cannot really say anything other than that.

Before long, we reached the first section of scree and I can honestly say this is the worst part. It may not look it from the road by the opposite shore but this part of the scree (right hand side as you face the screes) is made up of large boulders and there is no clear path across them. You have to make your way carefully between rocks, using your hands as well as feet and trying and keep a broadly straight line to the other side. It is not as easy as it sounds because the varying sizes of boulders and places to put your feet do not send you in a convenient straight line and because the curve of the scree is convex, you cannot see where you are heading. The lake below gives you a good measuring point, however. When you look down to the lake (because you will not be able to resist it) you can see the scree just carries on right into the water and presumably down to the bottom of the lake. It looks dark and very deep, but helps to focus the mind on not falling in! The water is about 10 to 15 feet down at this point.

We emerged, with relief, more by luck than judgement onto the path at the opposite side of the scree. The path then is more obvious and you can continue to enjoy the views. My eyes kept being drawn to the crags, rocks and scree above – they are mesmerising. The path in between screes is fairly straightforward and the next section of scree we arrived at was made up of smaller rocks and we could identify a path. Hands were required less for this part, although passing people coming the other way can be tricky in places so be considerate (especially if the other person looks more scared than you!) On we went and after several other scree sections of the same nature – tricky in places but with identified paths – finished the scree. The path opens up towards the other end of the lake towards the farm and you end up walking through grassy fields next to the shore. The views at this point at close range to the Scafells and Lingmell are as lovely as you would expect, as well across the lake to Yewbarrow and towards Great Gable and Kirk Fell at Wasdale Head.

The second half of the walk is straightforward and once you get to the road, you just follow it back to along the shore at the foot of Yewbarrow and Middle Fell.

When we had finished the walk, it felt like we had really achieved something special. I had thought it was going to be much easier than it was, but at six miles you feel like you have done something greater and you have – you have conquered the Wastwater screes!

There are many other low-level walks and many guide books out there with suggestions and maps. Most bed and breakfasts, hotels and self-catering cottages will also have information on local walks for those staying and there is a wealth of information online. I do urge anyone who has not walked in the Lakes before to ensure they are clear about the route and what is involved, however, before venturing out. I have seen too many people underestimate walks.

Tarns
Lake District tarns are part of its glacial history. Most were formed when glaciers tore out rocks, leaving hollows that then filled with melting snow and ice and continue to be fed by

run-off from the surrounding hills. Some of them in turn feed larger lakes in the valleys. There are countless tarns in the Lake District, some of the more famous being Tarn Howes (an original tarn made larger and landscaped), Angle Tarn, Loughrigg Tarn, Easedale Tarn, Allcock Tarn, Sprinkling Tarn, Styhead Tarn and Stickle Tarn (breathtaking) – there are also many others.

My very first solitary walk in the Lake District was to Easedale Tarn near Grasmere. It was in the spring (March, from memory) and it was an eerie day with low mist in the valley. I took the Easedale road from Grasmere, which also heads towards Helm Crag, and then crossed a bridge on the left to head towards Easedale Tarn. It was a lovely walk with an excellent path throughout and while quite steep in places, there was nothing particularly strenuous. The cascades of Sour Milk Gill were at their very best as there had been a lot of rain recently – you could see why the 'milk' reference came about as the water was a beautiful bright white as it came over the cascades.

From the cascades, the tarn is very close and I had one of those moments when it came in sight through the mist where I just said 'Wow!'. I have had many of those moments in the Lake District. Seeing Easedale Tarn in the mist, with the peak of Belles Knott behind it and the ghostly slopes of Tarn Crag and Blea Rigg each side, felt a little bit scary. I was all alone in the mountain scenery with only the sound of the cascades in the distance and the occasional bird. The water was as still as ice. I stood there for a long time and felt really liberated that I had done this walk on my own. It may not seem much to those who walk alone a lot, but this was a new experience for me and it was one I can remember as though it were yesterday.

I returned to Grasmere via the Far Easedale valley. This involved a very careful balancing act across the foot of Easedale Tarn on some stepping stones that were too far apart and too wet at that time of year. I managed to scramble across without incident and headed down the other side of Sour Milk Gill to join the Helm Crag path back to Grasmere. On the way, I came across a couple who had come from Grasmere to climb Helm Crag but had missed the turning so were heading towards Far Easedale. I managed to steer them back in the right direction and onto the correct path. Get me! Not just brave enough to walk alone but also assisting others with navigation! My geography teacher would never believe it!

If you go on any mountain walk, the chances are you will see a tarn or two on the way – some of which are named but many are not as they are too small or come and go depending on the weather. Wainwright himself had his ashes scattered near Innominate Tarn on Haystacks. Some of my favourites are Stickle Tarn (Langdale), Alcock Tarn (near Grasmere), Bleaberry Tarn (near Buttermere) and Angle Tarn near Patterdale. When planning a walk, if you can plan a route that includes a tarn or two then it adds to the experience, in my view. On some walks you will find them anyway even without planning to.

Low fells

Size is not everything. As well as low level walks if you want to avoid the fells altogether, there are several low fells that are wonderful to climb and that give you a real sense of being

Helm Crag – true summit is the Howitzer.

on or among mountains. Some of them give an experience and views that could compete with many of the higher fells.

A classic fell that falls into this category is **Castle Crag**. This is the fell I took my friend's family up in August 2011 and they loved it. This fell truly has the attributes of a much larger fell, yet from Grange is only 700 feet/213 metres of ascent over one and a half miles.

If you want to avoid a scramble then there are two fells that spring instantly to mind. The first is **Binsey**. Who could not love this grassy dome that marks the most northern fell in the Wainwright series? It stands proudly on its own looking out to sea and back into the Lake District. A grassy, easy path from Binsey Lodge takes you to the summit cairn in only a mile ascending 620 feet/189 metres where the best view is the back of the Skiddaw range that many visitors to the Lake District never see. Binsey was the 100th Wainwright fell I climbed and I chose it for that reason, so it will always be special to me. This is one you could pretty much do in heels (or flip flops at least!)

The other fell is **Hallin Fell**, with an ascent starting from the church of St Peter's at Martindale. A mere stroll up a grassy path takes you to one of the largest summit cairns (3.6 metres high) and views along Ullswater that are breathtaking.

Me scaling the Howitzer.

More centrally located low fells are also available. Two of the best fells to climb from Grasmere, whether you are looking for a low fell or not, are Loughrigg and Helm Crag. These are more strenuous than the previously mentioned fells, but still highly manageable.

Loughrigg is a wide, quite lumpy fell that provides the back drop to Grasmere and Rydal Water and can be seen clearly from the road linking to two. The shortest way up Loughrigg is from Red Bank, but from Grasmere is a lovely climb with 920 feet/280 metres of ascent over two and a quarter miles. A large cairn known as the Grasmere Cairn lets you know you are almost at the top. From the summit you can see the Langdale Pikes, Coniston Fells, up the valley to Dunmail Raise and Skiddaw beyond and also parts of the Hellelyn range and Fairfield Horseshoe. The photo on the front cover of this book is from my first time on Loughrigg. The mist in the valley below was mesmerising.

Helm Crag must tempt nearly everyone that passes it on the Grasmere to Keswick road. It is also popularly known as the Lion and the Lamb owing to the shape the rocks make on the Grasmere side of the summit. From Grasmere it is 1,100 feet/335 metres of ascent over one and a half miles. Whilst steep in places, there is not anything too challenging until you reach the top. The true top is the Howitzer – a large rock standing at over nine metres tall on the summit. I have climbed the Lion but not the Howitzer – at two-thirds of the way up, I decided retreat was the better part of valour – it is on my 'to do' list.

High Rigg from St John's in the Vale church (a short distance from the A591 near Thirlmere) is a very short ascent and again, has great views. If you are feeling energetic, then the way to get the most out of this walk is to include Low Rigg and Tewet Tarn. There is an interesting link with St John's in the Vale and Haweswater. When Haweswater dam was being constructed, the Manchester Corporation housed many of the workers in the purpose-built village of Burnbanks just below the dam. A Mission Church was also constructed as part of this. When the dam was complete and the workers left to find jobs elsewhere, Manchester Corporation dismantled the Mission building and reconstructed it in St John's in the Vale, where, to this day, it is still the Parish Hall for that parish and Wythburn. An early form of recycling?!

Black Fell (also known as Black Crag) is another popular low fell and well worth a climb. The paths are good as are the views and the route is fairly straightforward. You can climb this fell from a range of places; we did it from Sunny Brow near Barngates (near Ambleside). It has the added advantage of being extremely close to the Drunken Duck Inn, which provides an excellent lunch stop afterwards!

Perhaps one of my favourite lower fells (unexpectedly so) is **Troutbeck Tongue**. The best route is from Troutbeck (Queen's Head area). While there is quite a long walk along a narrow lane to get to the start of the climb, it is very pleasant and a good warm-up! When I did this walk, I saw a beautiful deer with the most amazing antlers walk out on one of the ledges higher up the fell. He looked all around him as though he was master of all he surveyed and then sauntered back the way he had come. It was an amazing sight! The climb was straightforward (make sure you take the left path immediately beyond the wall, not before it – it is hard to identify) and the views, whilst restricted owing to the larger fells around, are lovely to Windermere and I just loved it there. It is about two miles to the summit from the Queen's Head and approximately 500 feet/152 metres of ascent.

A selection of others include: Sale Fell from the Wythop Valley near Bassenthwaite Lake; Rannerdale Knotts from Crummock Water; Whinlatter from the Grizedale Forest visitor centre; Holme Fell from Yew Tree Tarn near Coniston; Great Mell Fell and Little Mell Fell near Ullswater; and Gowbarrow Fell from the top of Aira Force waterfall. They are all very different but all give you a sense in one way or another of the Lake District.

Chapter Eleven: No Such Thing as Bad Weather?

As the English writer and critic of art and architecture, John Ruskin said:

'Sunshine is delicious, rain is refreshing, wind braces us up, snow is exhilarating: there is really no such thing as bad weather, only different kinds of good weather'.

There are plenty of holidays you can go on where you can pretty much guarantee the weather is going to be sunny and warm. I have had holidays like that with friends in the Greek Islands and Ballearics, and with my husband on honeymoon in Antigua. It is rather more hit and miss in the English Lake District, but personally I think that adds to its charm. I love the Lake District in all weather and I have climbed fells in all types of weather as well. It looks beautiful in the sunshine and in the snow, but there is something eerie and beautiful about the fells in the rain or mist when you cannot see very far. The Lakes is full of micro climates – you can be in one valley in the sunshine and over in the next valley, it is raining. The distinctions are even more apparent when you are on the top of mountains and looking into two valleys – the variations are amazing.

The clouds are also amazing. I have already written about the cloud inversion I experienced when climbing Steel Fell, but there have been many other occasions where the clouds have really added to the beauty of the Lakes – the Wastwater area in particular in my view, when there are wispy clouds at the top of the lake over Great Gable and Yewbarrow.

On a recent climb up Scafell from Wastwater, the first third of the climb gave amazing views over the lake and to the fells beyond with just a touch of snow visible. But after climbing another thousand feet or so, we were in clouds and the ice formations on the rocks were simply stunning. The wind shelter was also completely full of snow! When you compare the view from the valley and the snow and ice at the top, you would think they were from different walks, but I promise it was the same day and the same walk!

I was in the Lakes for a few days in September 2011 and it was a week of total contrasts. On Sunday it was windy and so wet on top of Hartsop Dodd that I could not even look at the view in one direction because the hailstones were so ferocious! I did manage to see some views, however, on the way up, albeit misty ones. On Monday, the tail end of Hurricane Katia meant I took the decision not to climb at all (although some people did). There were still strong winds on Tuesday on the way up Wetherlam and a couple who were on the same route turned back, but I battled on taking extra care. The wind had gone by Wednesday but the rain meant the top of Fleetwith Pike was too cold to

Green Crag – like a desolate moon.

Icy rocks.

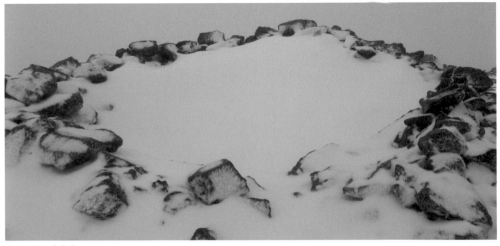

Snowy wind shelter.

stay on too long and the mist lingered on Great Gable in the parallel ridge. However, by Thursday I was basking in the sunshine in a t-shirt on the top of Seathwaite Fell and later Hencomb! Seathwaite is apparently the wettest inhabited part of the Lake District, so that was even more bizarre.

The same was true when I climbed my final five Wainwright's. I had the most glorious weather imaginable for March, wearing factor 50 suncream (and still burning my nose!) and in a t-shirt the whole time. The following week (when I had returned to the south east) it snowed in the Lake District! I cannot help but love English weather! After all, if it did not behave so bizarrely, what would we talk about?

The difference in weather creates different types of magic in the Lakes – sometimes the lakes are so still you can see the fells reflected in them like a mirror; at other times it is as though the waves are dancing on the shore edges. The mountains are breathtaking in sunshine with blue skies, but when they are covered in snow they are simply beautiful.

The weather is part of the charm of the Lake District and I have been lucky enough to see it in all weather and in all seasons. It is also fabulous sitting in a cosy pub with a warm fire and a glass of red wine with the snow falling outside, and just as wonderful sitting outside overlooking the fells in the sunshine while sipping a glass of very chilled white wine. It is just a magical place whatever the weather (although, yes, I would take a little more sunshine if it was offered!)

Here are some examples of the less sunny side of the Lake District weather (but I loved it anyway).

A very windy time!
Hartsop Dodd and Hurriance Katia
This was my 191st Wainwright, but there were two firsts for me.

I left Sussex at about 4.30am and arrived in Hartsop around 10am (after a quick nap and bacon sandwich at the Norton Canes services in Birmingham). It was tipping it down in Sussex but from the M40 all the way to Hartsop, it was dry and once the sun rose, it was shining. It is usually the other way around! Then, true to form, as soon as I got out of the car the rain began. Oh well, a little rain never deterred me! I was fully equipped with waterproofs and a pair of new fast-dry trousers that I had only used a couple of times before. This was their first time in rain. They had proved excellent in the hot sun a few weeks before, keeping cool and in the cold wind, keeping warm.

Hartsop Dodd stands at 2,028 feet/618 metres and there is about 1,500 feet/457 metres of ascent from Hartsop over about a mile in distance. It has been one I have meant to climb for a while as I have passed it a lot going over the Kirkstone Pass. It stands right in front of you as you head towards Ambleside from Ullswater challenging you to climb it. I wanted just a single mountain after my drive so it was perfect.

Off I set! It starts going up right at the beginning and then just gets steeper! Now, I have to say that every mountain you climb has steep bits and some longer than others, but this was relentlessly steep the whole way up. This was not unexpected, as it is clear from looking at it and looking at the maps that while not the biggest mountain, it is a challenge. It afforded me lots of opportunities for view stops though, which despite the rain, were quite good. There was another solitary walker ahead of me and I sometimes find this depressing (must be the competitive part of me); it was particularly so in this case as he just highlighted how very steep the route ahead was. It is also not an ideal time to keep checking the GPS as – as I've explained before – the steepness means it looks like you are standing still!

I was doing well and making good progress. The rain was getting heavier and the wind was picking up, but you could still see the surrounding mountains of Grey Crag and Brock Crags, with The Knott and High Street behind and over the other valley, Hartsop Above How leading to Hart Crag. I could also see the head of Ullswater. There were also other walkers behind me just starting the steep ascent (this always cheers me up as I can revel in the fact I have done more of the hard work than they have... this says something about me I am sure but I will not dwell on that!) At this point I learned something – my trousers, while fabulous in many ways, were *not* waterproof! They were simply soaked. They may be fast-drying but when the rain does not let up that is not helpful. It was too late to bother with my waterproof over-trousers so I stuck it out. Note to self for the future though – there is no escaping waterproof over-trousers, however un-elegant they are!

As I approached the top (shoulders going back by now as I was nearly there and as ever, the pounding heart on the way up forgotten) the wind became a quite severe gale and the rain turned to hail. Apparently, the north of England was suffering the tail-end of Hurricane Katia, which had battered the east coast of America at the end of August. Gales and hail! What fun! These were two firsts for me (and I would not be disappointed if they were lasts as well!). My stay on the top was brief as a result and back down I went, smiling at all the people on their way up and feeling very virtuous! It only took about half an hour to get back to the car. Then the fun started – getting changed out of my wet-through trousers and dripping waterproof jacket with my boot full of luggage for the week ahead. Now here, I confess, I lost the elegance I try to achieve while climbing. Wet socks and trousers everywhere (slightly muddy too owing to a slip near the final gate that I will gloss over). I also had to discard my usual determination of avoiding muddy and wet boots making my car dirty and just chuck it all in. Sometimes, a girl has to do what a girl has to do for the sake of climbing mountains!

Let it snow!

Lakeland is beautiful when the mountains are snow-capped. In some ways, it is even better than in sunshine,

Robin in snow.

so winter has become one of my favourite times to be there. The snow on the fells and the cold crisp air brings an even greater magical quality to it than in the summer, in my view. The first time I visited the Lakes in winter was in December 2008. Waking up one morning to see Skiddaw covered in snow was simply breathtaking and I fell in love with the Lakes all over again. Snow can also add a little extra frisson to fell-walking, as I found out!

It was December 2010. Snow lay all around but it was a bright sunny day – perfect for a winter climb (although my husband, Paul, was less convinced)! I chose the Red Screes and then a route onto Middle Dodd, Little Hart Crag and High Hartsop Dodd, with the starting point being the top of the Kirkstone Pass opposite the pub (not that I had the end of the walk in mind at all). It all started well. We were dressed in thermals, ski jackets, snoods, hats, gloves – the whole kit and caboodle (obviously I was in pink). Paul had two walking poles (he is a true advocate of them – I am less so). I had spent a long time mapping the route and was confident of the paths. Up we went on a clear path and while it was icy and care was needed, it was straightforward climbing. However, nearer the top, owing to the deep snow, the path became less clear. This was not unexpected as it can happen in those types of conditions, but we knew from the GPS that we were heading in the right direction. I should also say at this point that I know what I am doing on mountains. I do not take risks and despite my sometimes flaky, over-positive nature in life, I am highly organised and sensible on the fells – I am my father's daughter. But everyone is human and we can make errors. For a few minutes, we had been following footsteps as someone had clearly been there before us that morning (or certainly since the last snow fall). However, these footprints then veered up to the left, whereas I was certain (after consulting the Ordnance Survey and GPS) that the path lay straight on up a more gentle slope. Paul was certain these footsteps were a shortcut. My instincts at this point were to stick with the path and what our map tools were telling us – that is one of the key rules of mountain climbing. However, there did not seem to be any harm, given how clear the weather was, to vary the route a little. So up the steeper snow-covered slope we went. What could possibly go wrong?

After a few minutes, I started to have doubts – after all, how did we know the owner of the footprints was going the same way we wanted to go? It is always better to stick to a path and not go off-piste and I absolutely knew that and usually live by that rule. Then, as the footprints started to go up a snowy gully, I noticed an enormous hole in the snow – the guy we were following had obviously also discovered it as the hole was leg-shaped. I peered in cautiously, wondering whether our footprint guide was down there somewhere. I could not see him and it was not very deep so I decided on balance he was probably not there. It was a long stretch to get to the rocks on the other side however so I turned to Paul with a 'What do we do now?' look. Given the 'shortcut' idea had been his idea he pretended to study the snow intensely. In order to get across the hole I had to take a leap from my one firm footing onto my knee onto the rock the other side – I did not want to step on the snow as I did not know if it was firm or whether there was another gully underneath. Now, I have long legs and I thank Mother Nature for this every time I am in the Lakes. I managed to stretch across. I will also admit at this point that the manoeuvre was far from elegant and anyone handing our marks out of 10 for finesse would have been looking for the 'minus' symbol.

Paul could have been on a beach in Barbados.

In the pink on the summit of Scafell.

Ice on Seat Sandal.

Once across and nursing my dignity, I turned around and saw Paul attempting the same manoeuvre. It is actually worse watching someone else as there is nothing you can do to help and he was struggling with the two walking poles (clearly not dropping those down the steep drop was more important than his own safety – that or he did not want to have to buy new ones). In situations like this, I prefer to have my hands free to scramble and cling onto things, which is why I do not use poles very often. I use any part of my anatomy that I feel can help – all those 'legs, bums and tums' aerobics classes were starting to pay off!

Anyway – with poles around his ears and tangled in his legs, he eventually got onto the safety of the rocks as well. 'Well', I said, 'that was exciting'. Paul looked at me with the 'I could be on a beach in Barbados' look, so I swiftly moved on.

We managed to reach the top without further adventure. At the top of the snowy gully, the footprints continued but I ignored those in favour of what the GPS said. A valuable couple of lessons learned though. First, never trust a man over a satellite or Ordnance Survey system and second, never follow random footprints in the snow! You never know where they lead! I say this even as an experienced walker as it just goes to show that anyone can make wrong decisions.

Scafell by sledge

The Red Screes experience was merely the beginning of my snow-climbing. Another amazing snow experience for quite different reasons was on Scafell. You would not believe from the photos taken at the beginning of this walk that it was the same day as the ones from the top. Whilst sometimes a reluctant climber as you know, my husband was looking forward to this climb as it was a 'proper' mountain, so he came on this walk with enthusiasm and whilst it did not become one of his favourites, it was very memorable. We took the Greenhow route, which is not the most exciting route up Scafell but given we thought there may be snow on top, we wanted to be careful (yes, it is still me writing – I do learn lessons after all it seems!)

The views across Wastwater and to the fells across the water to Yewbarrow, Middle Fell and Kirk Fell were amazing. After walking up the grassy path for about an hour, we started to reach the cloud and snow and a few minutes later we were enveloped in mist. We kept walking and started to feel we must be nearing the summit as we had been walking quite a while. However, at that point, the mist cleared briefly and ahead, was a large looming mass that looked like a whole separate fell, but was in fact the rest of Scafell. How depressing! Paul was a few feet behind and had not looked at the sight but when he did, his reaction was, 'We don't have to climb that do we?!' Um... how to break the news? 'Yes I think we do but I am sure it is not as bad as it looks!'. Sometimes optimism can be infuriating and this was one of those moments. Sometimes, a person's face tells you a lot more about what they are thinking than their words. I will not share the words.

The snow got deeper and the path got rockier and it took a lot of energy, especially when our legs sank to our knees in the snow, but at least it was not as tiring as Kirk Fell. The snow and ice patterns on the rocks near the top were simply stunning – the wind had blown the snow and it had frozen in patterns that looked like they had come from another planet. When we reached the summit, the wind shelter was filled with snow! It was like a different day to the beautiful views across Waterwater from lower down the fell. We could not see anything, although I believe the views to Scafell Pike are striking from there! I pointed out the mountains we should have been looking at to Paul and I got the 'look' again so we sat down and poured the coffee and had something to eat. It was a real shame that there were no views but to be sitting on the second highest mountain in the Lake District was special anyway and at that point, it was the highest fell I had climbed.

We took the opposite route down towards Slight Side and the snow was still deep. I admit I was getting rather tired of my legs falling into the snow and not being able to take a step without having to pull my leg from a foot of snow! So I thought back to my descent of Kirk Fell and thought, 'Well, we could sledge down in our ski trousers!'. So we did! The slope was wide and not very steep so it felt very safe and down we went. It was such incredible fun – it is the first time I have got down part of a mountain and wanted to walk back up and do it again! Slight Side was a strange mountain and felt like a part of Scafell rather than a separate fell. It is mainly a large rock for a summit and not something you can spend much time on comfortably. We continued our walk down as it was too cold to spend any time there anyway. We emerged from the mist and snow and had delightful views to Harter Fell (Eskdale) and towards the Coniston fells. A long winding path across quite a marshy area saw us arrive near Boot where mum and dad picked us up and took us back to Wasdale.

A swift shandy for me and pint of bitter for Paul in Nether Wasdale was a perfect reward for a long walk. Scafell will forever be in my head as the fell I sledged down in my ski trousers. I look forward to doing that again one day!

Seat Sandal

I have other wonderful memories of climbing mountains in the snow now – December visits are a compulsory part of my year! To see my favourite view down Wasdale with snow-capped mountains is so different from seeing it in sunshine – both are beautiful.

So it was that in December 2010 I parked on the top of Dunmail Raise ready to tackle a lone fell – Seat Sandal. Yes, even shoes get a mention in the names of fells – it was meant to be, like the mother ship calling me home! There is a large cairn in the middle of the dual carriageway on the top of Dunmail Raise and it is thought by some to mark the burial ground of Dunmail, King of Cumbria. However, others argue that as it sits on the boundary between the two old counties of Westmorland and Cumberland, it is merely a boundary mark. If I am totally honest, having been visiting the Lake District for over 30 years from a baby, I only noticed the cairn about four years ago! If any of you have never noticed it, look out for it next time – it is enormous! For those of you who have noticed it, my excuse is there are much prettier sights to be looking at from that point!

The temperature at that height (780 feet/238 metres) was –5 degrees centigrade. Pretty chilly, and it was only going to get more chilly on top as Seat Sandal is 2,415 feet/736

Grisedale Tarn.

Sometimes you don't know how deep the snow is!

metres and a brisk breeze was blowing! I was fully kitted out, however, and feeling quite toastie. The initial ascent up Raise Beck was steep in places but was a lovely rocky scramble next to a stream with the sound of water cascading down the valley and everything was just white. There were no footprints in the snow – I was the first up the path that day (most sensible people being somewhere much warmer I imagine!). I have been up the Raise Beck route before, when I climbed the Hellvelyn range from Dollywagon Pike to Clough Head (I just love the names of the fells!), but in rather milder conditions!

The sights to see were incredible – there were icicles everywhere and frozen puddles, mini water-falls and snow sweeping away like glossy meringue (although the meringue I make usually looks more grainy... but I live in hope that my actual domestic goddess skills will catch up with the creations in my head one day). I was enjoying the climb enormously and then I emerged from the rocky valley into an opening and a beautiful view to a frozen Grisedale Tarn with St Sunday Crag behind. This was an incredibly pretty sight and to have it all to myself was amazing. There was not a soul around – it was a silent tarn protected by white giants.

The final climb to the summit of Seat Sandal was short but steep next to a broken wall and it was getting colder by the minute. At the top, however, with the cairn standing proudly on the round summit, every thought of cold was pushed from my head as the vista in all directions was perfect – crisp, snowy mountains rolled on for miles and miles with a blue sky, barely a white cloud in sight and the sun simply dazzling. It never ceases to amaze me how beautiful the Lake District is and how lucky I was to see it like this.

I found a rock to sit on and at that point I took my water out of my rucksack to find it had frozen! It was literally a block of ice – it had been fine when I got out of the car but between the car and the top, it had almost totally solidified. My hair poking out my hat and coat, which must have gathered moisture on the way up, was crunchy with ice and had tiny icicles hanging off it! That had never happened before. I did not stop long on the top as while it was beautiful, it was absolutely freezing and I was starting to lose feeling in my toes and fingers. I went back down the same way – the steep part back down to Grisedale Tarn saw me zig-zagging across the slope to avoid slipping down! Given my knowledge now about how effective ski-trousers are for sledging (gathered from my Scafell climb), I would have sledged down instead!

It was a relief to get back to the car and the warm! From Dunmail Raise, I was quite close to one of my favourite haunts, The Drunken Duck at Barngates, so that was my lunch stop of choice. Legend has it (if you believe the story on the wall in the pub itself) that the name 'The Drunken Duck' came about because a landlady in Victorian times found her ducks lying in the road and she believed them to be dead. She promptly plucked them ready for dinner but it turned out they were actually drunk rather than dead as a result of beer from the cellar having leaked into their feeding ditch. The landlady, full of guilt for having plucked them, knitted them waistcoats until their feathers grew back! Whether that is true or not, it is a fantastic story!

So, sunshine is not always necessary – the Lake District is beautiful in all weather

A snowy Lake District scene.

Chapter Twelve: The Wainwright's and Me

Why did I climb all the Wainwright's?

Some people can be very dismissive of those trying to climb all the Wainwright's (or indeed any named group of fells). 'Peak bagging' is not always used as a compliment. Others think it is crazy to climb 214 mountains – why would anyone put themselves through that? So I thought it was important to capture why I did it.

To start with, it was never my original intention to climb them all. The seven Wainwright books had been on mum and dad's bookshelves for as long as I could remember. They were faded and worn so obviously they were well used. When I first started going to the Lake District as an adult, I usually kept to low-level walks or short mountain walks and enjoyed that, but had no urge to climb bigger mountains or climb lots of mountains.

I bought the Wainwright books (revised versions by Chris Jesty) in March 2009 when only books one to six were completed. I saw them on the bookshelf in Hawkshead and as I flicked through the pages they caught my imagination. What amazing drawings and such detail! I loved the context and the history of the introductions for each fell. I had always wanted to know what the mountains were called and recognise them when I saw them like my dad could. This looked the perfect way to help me start to recognise them. I made an impulse purchase of all six there and then and left the shop well pleased!

That evening I started reading Book Six – the North Western Fells – and I liked the sound of Robinson. It was such an unusual name for a mountain and it looked manageable on my own, so I decided I would climb it the next day. And I did. I loved it and wrote in the chapter in the book the month and year I climbed it. I decided it would be nice to climb a few of the Wainwright's. And I did that too. The next holiday saw me on Brock Crags, Angletarn Pikes and various other fells and each time I wrote in the book the month and year. I was enjoying this challenge enormously: it was taking me to parts of the Lake District I had never been to before and I was climbing mountains I had never previously heard of. I was even climbing fells my mum and dad had not done. I was also starting to understand the geography of the Lake District better and know how all the fells linked together and the areas they were in. I could therefore could recognise more of them when I saw them from the roads and valleys, as well as from the summits and ridges.

A glimmer in my thoughts one day turned into a beacon and I thought – well, why don't I try and climb them all? That way I would go to some of the remotest parts of the Lake District, learn even more about the geography and find some fabulous routes, secret places,

Great Gable from Lingmell.

A busy Scafell Pike summit.

Sprinkling Tarn.

tarns, streams, rocks, crags and sights that I would never see anywhere else. So I decided to do it! I thought I would achieve it by the time I was 40. A change in career in 2011 meant I had more flexibility and could go to the Lakes more often and therefore I completed them before the age of 35. I climbed Robinson in March 2009. By March 2012, all 214 were complete and I was right – I had been to some wonderful places.

I began keeping a journal in 2010 after being given Wainwright's *A Walker's Notebook* (2007) as a birthday gift. I have enjoyed keeping the journal and it has helped me enormously as I came to write this book, even though I only began writing it for my own amusement.

A Great End!

When I had about 20 Wainwright mountains still to climb I realised the one called 'Great End' was still on the list, so I decided that had to be the right mountain to end my challenge on. Probably not an original idea, but it seemed fitting. As it turned out, it could not have been more true! I was lucky enough to be in the Lake District at the end of March 2012 during the unseasonal warm sunshine that lasted over a week. I was truly blessed to be able to complete my mission in some of the most amazing conditions.

Sunset over Wastwater.

I arrived on Sunday and as a warm-up, headed up Loughrigg Fell from Red Bank (as you do) and stayed in Elterwater. On Monday, I was up early and off to Ennerdale to undertake Caw Fell and Haycock. Haycock has made it into my top 10 fells so I will not duplicate that wonderful walk here, but instead will turn straight to Tuesday and my final three fells of Lingmell, Scafell Pike and Great End. I was staying in Grasmere by then and travelled to Wasdale Head to start the climb. I totally underestimated how long it would take me to get to Wasdale Head from Grasmere so I did not start climbing until 10.30am, which is very late for me. I was not alone – there were several groups, couples and individuals on the same route as me and it was nice to have people around on such a glorious day. Wastwater looked

divine in the sunshine and, of course, for the first part of the walk I could see Yewbarrow (my favourite fell) so my spirits were high! I was a recognisable addition to the fells that day with my purple and white striped hat.

I took the popular Brown Tongue route to Lingmell. It was hard work I have to say, and very hot (a nice problem to have overall!) with the local Fix the Fells team's work evident for much of the route in the rocky steps they had created. Much of the walk followed Lingmell Beck and hearing the stream run gently over the rocks was wonderful. The higher up I got, the more I could see the crags between Scafell and Scafell Pike on my right looking

Sour Milk Gill.

extremely menacing but awe-inspiring. Once I reached the ridge, however, my route took me to the left up the final pull to Lingmell. I could tell my fitness levels were somewhat improved from the Fairfield Horseshoe in February as I overtook people! I had spent a lot of time at the gym in the preceding weeks for just this occasion and all that time on the stepping machine was finally paying off!

However, as I looked up the last steep bit to the summit of Lingmell, I admit I had to draw breath and psyche myself up as it looked horrendous! That was until I looked to the right, however, and saw what was going to be the last part of the route to Scafell Pike, which was about three times as long and three times as steep! How was I ever going to get up that? I focused on Lingmell first, and started the unforgiving final ascent. The summit made it all worth it – the views across to Great Gable and the Mosedale Horseshoe were stunning, with Great Gable looking like the perfect mountain peak but with an eroded red scar all the way down the edge. The rocks and crags below on Lingmell were magnificent and the view to Scafell Pike and Scafell in such close proximity with Mickledore in between was wonderful. Here on this fell it felt great to be alive and all the effort it had taken to get there was forgotten.

That was until I looked back to Scafell Pike and the full extent of the next part of the route. No – that had not started to look any easier. It would have been hard enough from the level I was at but I had to drop back down to the dip before starting the ascent. Wainwright says in his book that it takes about half an hour to get to Scafell Pike from Lingmell and he describes it as 'tedious'. That was hardly inspiring and it looked like it would take a lot longer than half an hour to me, but after another deep breath off I went to conquer the highest mountain in England.

I was right – the final part of the ascent to Scafell Pike was horrible! There were lots of people coming down as it was early afternoon by this point and that actually did not look a lot easier as the route was covered in boulders and loose rocks that meant any wrong footing could prove costly! At one point I found a patch of shade next to an enormous boulder and virtually hugged the boulder so I could be in the shade for a few minutes! I kept going, knowing each step was taking me closer to the summit. As I got nearer to the distinctive top the ground flattened out as I hopped from boulder to boulder. Then, suddenly, I was there and on the summit of Scafell Pike! Hurrah! I had done it!

It was the busiest summit I had ever been on with about 30 or 40 people up there, but at that moment it mattered little as the euphoria of making it was just wonderful! The views were outstanding, with rugged mountains stretching out for miles and miles. It was exhilarating to be there.

If I am being objective, it is far from the best summit I have been on and it looked like every single boulder in the country had been collected and dropped in the square mile surrounding the summit. I do not mind sharing summits with fellow walkers and it is nice to pass the time of day with new people but this could have passed for Kings Cross Station! As for it taking half an hour from Lingmell, well, I know I am not the fittest person in the world, nor am I the slowest but it still took 50 minutes. Wainwright must have been super human! However, none of that mattered as I was on the highest point in England with only one fell to go to complete my mission. Stretching out before me was the route to Great End between Broad Crag and Ill Crag, so after a quick sandwich and further admiring of views, off I went!

If I thought the route I took to Scafell Pike was hard then it was nothing compared to the route from the Borrowdale direction. I had to descend a route with as many boulders and rocks as on the way up, but this descent looked even longer and steeper so I felt for those people on their way up! The boulder graveyard continued for the whole route and I confess at this point that even though I was so close, I could not face the summits of Broad Crag and Ill Crag (not classed as separate Wainwright's but if you can include them then do). Great End was then just a stone's throw away and only a short climb.

The last 10 minutes walking to the summit I had butterflies in my tummy as I was feeling so excited about ending my mission. It felt really momentous and I cannot really articulate why other than to say that while I may not be a typical climber (if such a person exists) – some of my routes and methods climbing the fells were unorthodox, and I have made mistakes and been lucky on occasions – I felt a real sense of achievement. I had conquered 214 fells, living over 300 miles away from them. I had climbed in snow, mist, wind, rain, hail, sleet and beautiful sunshine. I had climbed on my own, as a couple and with a family. I had seen views and felt emotions I did not know were possible and here at this moment on this mountain I felt I could take on the world and win. As I touched the cairn, the euphoria was overwhelming. I had done it. A truly great end on Great End.

I stood by the cairn taking it all in and enjoying the emotions. A few minutes later a man with a small terrier arrived on the summit and I just had to share my achievement with him. He was the first to congratulate me and shake my hand. I stayed on the summit for a while and then began my descent. I had chosen a route back to Wasdale that went via Sprinkling and Styhead Tarns via Esk Hause. The sun was still shining and it was lovely and warm. The walk back was a joy, with the sun shimmering on Sprinkling Tarn as I walked passed it and there were even people setting up to camp there (rather them than me – I was looking forward to a pub meal and a nice bed!). I was feeling pretty tired – I had been walking and climbing for eight hours, but a group of three men marched passed me at one point who did not look remotely tired – they looked like they could have popped up Scafell Pike again (and I bet they could have done it from Lingmell in half an hour!). The walk down the valley next to a stream between Great Gable on the right and Great End then Lingmell on the left was breathtaking and for the first time in my fell-walking history, as I approached the end of the walk back towards Wasdale Head, I saw the sun set over Wastwater and behind Yewbarrow. It was like heaven had opened up and extended its warm golden glow over my favourite part of the world and said 'you deserve a beautiful finish for a wonderful achievement'. Seeing my favourite lake, backed by my favourite mountain at the end of my mission was the best finish I could imagine. Splendid.

Onwards and upwards?!

I have a real sense of achievement about the 214. So what next? Well, I am not going to climb them all again that is for sure! There are some I would avoid like the plague but there

I did it!

are plenty I want to climb again in better weather (I am still an optimist) or from a different route. There are also other ridge walks I want to do. Some I want to do again exactly as I did them before. Some I want to take family and friends up (avoid all calls from me if you do not wish to be one of those people!).

I also want to explore new places – the National Parks in America and the mountains of Spain for example. I have not spent time in Scotland, and the Isle of Skye really appeals. There are lots of places I want to go but the Lake District will always be the place that I want to return to and I want to be able to climb there for as many years as my health will allow!

Epilogue

It has been a wonderful journey exploring the Lake District and I hope that journey continues for many years to come. Whilst there are other parts of the UK and indeed the world I want to explore, I find it hard to believe anywhere will surpass the Lake District. I also hope my combination of high heels and hills does not cause me too many knee problems as I get older! Perhaps it is a price I will have to pay at some point.

Some of the literary greats such as Beatrix Potter, Wordsworth, Coleridge, Keats and Arthur Ransome have immortalised the Lake District and Wainwright captured the magic and beauty of the mountains like no one before or since. Who could not fall in love with a place that has inspired such imagination? I have had a different approach to this book that is more light-hearted and hope I have brought alive the Lake District to a whole other group of people who perhaps have not been there before, and just maybe, I have added a little knowledge or at least given a laugh to those more experienced than me. You do not have to be a hardcore walker, climber, rock-climber or fitness fanatic to enjoy the Lake District. I am more determined than fit and perfectly happy to admit where I have got things wrong whilst exploring and the lessons I have learned. I hope some of those lessons help others but I suspect human nature means many of you will end up making the same mistakes. I have plenty more to make I am sure!

Since I started writing this book I have been trying to think of a really fantastic way to end it – something really gripping and momentous. I am still thinking what this fantastic ending might be so in the meantime, I will end as I began and turn to my leadership guru, Winnie-the-Pooh and use his words to capture how I feel when I leave the Lake District:

'How lucky I am to have something that makes saying goodbye so hard.'
Winnie-the-Pooh (A. A. Milne, 1926)

Looking to the future on Loughrigg.

References

Burgess P (2010) *Tubular Fells*. Available online at: www.tubularfells.com

Footprint Publishing (2002) *Walks Around Keswick: A map-guide including Borrowdale, Buttermere and Thirlmere*. Edinburgh: Footprint Publishing.

Milne A A (1928) *The House at Pooh Corner*. London: Methuen & Co. Ltd.

Milne A A (1926) *Winnie-the-Pooh*. London: Methuen & Co. Ltd.

Ransome A (1930) *Swallows and Amazons*. London: Jonathan Cape.

Rubery J & Law M (2011) *The Lakeland Pack 2*. Keighley: Orchard Publishing.

Wainwright A (1955-1966) *A Pictorial Guide to the Lakelands*, Books One to Seven: 'The Eastern Fells'; 'The Far Eastern Fells'; 'The Central Fells'; 'The Southern Fells'; 'The Northern Fells'; 'The North Western Fells'; 'The Western Fells'. Revised by Chris Jesty (2005-2009) London: Frances Lincoln.

Wainwright A (2007) *A Walker's Notebook*. London: Frances Lincoln.

Watson D (2009) *Making Sense of the Place Names of the Lake District*. Photoprint Scotland.

Bibliography

Beresford PJ (1993) *The Lakeland Pack*. Keighley: Orchard Publishing.

Lee A (2010) *Lake District Mountain Landscape*. London: Frances Lincoln.

Richards M (2008-11) Lakelander Fellranger series. Cumbria: Cicerone Press 'Ordnance Survey Explorer Maps' OL 4, 5, 6 and 7. Ordnance Survey.